Contents

Note: All economic statistics, such as those relating to GDP, employment, and trade, and agriculture's contribution to these, are based upon World Bank Development Indicators (World Bank 2005) unless otherwise stated. Similarly, unless otherwise stated, all agricultural production data are based on the FAOSTAT online database (http://faostat.fao.org, FAO 2004).

This is a print version of a report originally issued online as *Agricultural Trade Policy in Developing Countries During Take-Off* at
www.oxfam.org.uk/what_we_do/issues/trade/research_agricultural_trade.htm
The online report was uploaded in July 2006.
This print version, first published in January 2007, is the authoritative edition.

ISBN 978 0 85598 584 4

Oxfam GB

Oxfam GB, founded in 1942, is a development, humanitarian, and campaigning agency dedicated to finding lasting solutions to poverty and suffering around the world. Oxfam believes that every human being is entitled to a life of dignity and opportunity, and it works with others worldwide to make this become a reality.

From its base in Oxford in the United Kingdom, Oxfam GB publishes and distributes a wide range of books and other resource materials for development and relief workers, researchers and campaigners, schools and colleges, and the general public, as part of its programme of advocacy, education, and communications.

Oxfam GB is a member of Oxfam International, a confederation of 13 agencies of diverse cultures and languages which share a commitment to working for an end to injustice and poverty – both in long-term development work and at times of crisis.

For further information about Oxfam's publishing, and online ordering, visit www.oxfam.org.uk/publications

For information about Oxfam's development, advocacy, and humanitarian relief work around the world, visit www.oxfam.org.uk

Disclaimer

This Oxfam Research Report was written to inform policy development on trade issues and as a background paper for the Oxfam Poverty Report (forthcoming in 2008). It is published in order to share widely the results of Oxfam-commissioned research. The views expressed in the report are those of the author and do not necessarily reflect Oxfam's views

Acknowledgements

This paper was written by Michael Stockbridge, an independent consultant in agricultural economics, rural development, and the management of natural resources. Oxfam GB acknowledges the assistance of Duncan Green, Juan Cheaz, Craig Castro, Ashvin Dayal, Francis Perez and Steve Price-Thomas in its production. It is part of a series of papers written to inform public debate on development and humanitarian policy issues.

For further information on the issues raised in this paper please e-mail enquiries@oxfam.org.uk or go to www.oxfam.org.

Executive summary

Agricultural trade has always been one of the most sensitive international trade issues. Governments around the world have long been reluctant to abandon policy instruments that give them influence over domestic prices and allow them to raise revenues.

The most commonly cited justification for government intervention in agricultural trade is food security, since if domestic prices are too high, poor consumers may not be able to buy enough food, and if they are not high enough, producers will not produce enough food. The food security argument is stronger in some countries (e.g. food insecure developing countries) than in others (e.g. largely urbanised developed countries).

This study looks briefly at the agriculture and trade policies of six different developing countries, each of which has enjoyed unusually high rates of economic growth and development. They are South Korea, Malaysia, Indonesia, Viet Nam, Chile and Botswana. Their experience may shed further light on the extent to which governments should retain their powers to intervene in trade as opposed to relinquishing them in favour of market liberalisation.

Overall objectives of agriculture policy

Agriculture played a very large role in the economies of all of the countries prior to take-off, as a source of both GDP and employment. The exception is Chile, which began its process of urbanisation/industrialisation much earlier than other developing countries.

A common feature of agriculture in the Asian countries is the pivotal position of rice, mostly grown by relatively poor smallholders and therefore the main focus of policy-makers concerned with food security and poverty reduction. In Botswana, sorghum and maize play a similar role, and in Chile, wheat is the dominant crop.

In applying trade and other price-related policies, the six governments faced a trade-off between the welfare of producers on the one hand, and of consumers on the other. The six countries have approached this dilemma in different ways. South Korea favoured consumers over producers; in Malaysia and Indonesia policies have been generally supportive of rice producers; in Viet Nam, the government belatedly benefited rice producers by lifting export restraints; economic growth in Chile coincided with the liberalisation of both internal and external trade that served to eliminate the bias against agriculture; as a net importer of food Botswana kept domestic food prices under control by operating a liberal import regime, whilst at the same time using revenues from diamond exports to finance massive farm subsidies that helped to keep producer prices above their free market level.

One should not underestimate the importance of political stability in the pursuit of economic growth, nor the role of food and agricultural price stability in achieving this. Agricultural policy in many of the case study countries, especially the Asian ones, needs to be understood in this context.

Key policy instruments

A wide range of policy instruments have been used. In the staple food sector the Asian food-importing countries used state trading monopolies (Malaysia, Indonesia) and import licences and quotas (South Korea) – tariffs played a minimal role. In the other food-importing nations, food was either permitted to enter the country tariff-free (Botswana) or was subject to a variable levy aimed at stabilising domestic prices (Chile). Food-exporting nations (Viet Nam and Chile again) largely removed export restrictions, although both countries had placed heavy restrictions on trade prior to that. In Botswana a state-owned marketing board monopolised beef exports, whereas in Malaysia exports were carried out by the private sector and subject only to taxes.

In all of the case study countries except Chile, interventions in domestic markets typically involved state marketing boards that buy to defend a minimum support price for producers and sell to prevent consumer prices from exceeding a government-stipulated ceiling. The other important set of policy instruments relate to subsidised inputs and credit combined with public sector investment in rural infrastructure and agricultural research and extension.

Reducing price volatility, especially in rice, was a key aim of government action. Without such intervention consumers and producers (especially the poorer ones) would be very vulnerable to the peaks (consumers) and troughs (producers) of international price movements. Price stability combined with input and credit subsidies gave farmers the confidence and incentives to invest in the new more productive technologies of the Green Revolution.

Distributional impacts

In the Asian countries and in Botswana relatively poor smallholders are responsible for most staple food production. These producers have benefited from government support for the sector, although in Viet Nam these benefits were only fully realised when the government removed restrictions on rice exports. In a number of countries (Korea, Malaysia, and Botswana) there is very clear evidence of governments using the instruments of agricultural policy in an attempt to transfer resources from more prosperous parts of the economy to vulnerable groups in the rural sector (i.e. smallholders in the staple food sector). In Chile the situation is rather different. Large farms play a much bigger role in agricultural production than is the case in the other countries in the study. Consequently many of the direct benefits of agricultural liberalisation and export expansion have accrued to such farmers, largely bypassing rural smallholders.

Lessons for other developing countries

What lessons do the experiences of the case study countries provide for other developing countries? Caution is advisable in attempting to transfer lessons across countries – the Asian countries were uniquely suited to growing rice, for example, and conditions in Africa are much more hostile to irrigated agriculture. That said, the policies pursued by a number of the case study countries – Indonesia, Malaysia, and Korea – during economic take-off are clearly not consistent with the trade liberalisation agenda currently being promoted by the WTO and the international financial institutions.

Owing to the WTO's restrictions on other policy instruments such as subsidies and quotas, tariffs have become and will remain a much more important trade policy instrument than they were in the past. Currently, it seems as if developing countries will be allowed added flexibility in the use of tariffs on certain 'special products'. In the Doha Round, the number of commodities that can be designated as 'special' and the way they are to be treated is clearly an important negotiating issue.

Developing countries today face a very different international policy environment from that which existed when the economies of the countries in this study were beginning to take off. The flexibility of policy-makers in relation to trade policy is much more limited than it was 30 or 40 years ago. Smallholder development strategies of the sort pursued by the East Asian case study countries were underpinned by government use of trade policy instruments to influence domestic prices (protecting floor prices for farmers as well as ceiling prices for consumers). If less-developed countries today are to pursue similar strategies, they need to have a reasonable amount of flexibility in their use of duties and tariffs, since the much wider range of instruments that were available to governments prior to the Uruguay Round are no longer available.

The current liberalising agenda provides a fair amount of support for the sorts of strategies pursued by Chile, Botswana and, more recently, Viet Nam. However, developing countries wishing to follow the agricultural development strategies that were pursued by Korea, Malaysia, and Indonesia in previous decades may need more policy space than the current liberalising agenda would naturally wish to concede.

Overview

Introduction

Agricultural trade has always been and continues to be one of the most sensitive international trade issues. Governments around the world have long been reluctant to abandon policy instruments that give them control over the flow of agricultural commodities across their borders. This control is considered important because it allows governments to influence domestic prices and to raise revenues.

Food security

The most commonly cited justification for government intervention in agricultural trade is food security, since if domestic prices are too high, poor consumers may not be able to buy enough food, and if they are not high enough, producers will not produce enough food.

The food security argument is stronger in some countries than in others. In developed countries, for example, food represents only a small proportion of total expenditure, so trade-induced changes in the domestic price of food do not have a significant impact on the food security of individual consumers — not even the poorest of them, whose poverty lies in other forms of deprivation. In developing countries, where a much larger proportion of expenditure is devoted to food, the situation is quite different, since a rise in the price of basic food staples can very quickly threaten the food security of poor consumers. Similarly, the argument for supporting domestic food production through price and other incentives is weaker in rich countries which can easily afford to purchase food on the international market than in poor countries where foreign exchange earnings are often volatile and in short supply.

In developed countries where agriculture represents only a small proportion of GDP and employment, and where food security is no longer a pressing issue, the motivations for government intervention in agricultural trade – and for agricultural support more generally – are often more political than they are economic. They reflect the influence of powerful farm and agribusiness lobbies, combined with a broader concern to protect the rural way of life.

Agriculture and development

In developing countries, by contrast, agriculture plays a far greater role in the economy, both in terms of its contribution to national income and as a source of livelihood and employment for a large proportion of the population. Additionally, agricultural export revenues are often the main source of foreign exchange in developing countries, and intervention in trade may be one of the few reliable ways in which governments can raise revenues for public spending – in contrast with developed countries, which enjoy more sophisticated methods of tax collection.

Therefore, whilst agricultural sector intervention in developing countries is also highly political, its implications for the growth of the domestic economy and for the reduction of poverty are far greater than is the case in developed countries. Unfortunately, there is as yet no broad consensus about the precise nature of these implications. In the neoliberal economic view that informs the policies of the WTO, IMF, World Bank, and other international financial institutions, the drawbacks of government intervention are greater than the economic benefits of liberalising international and domestic markets. Yet many economists disagree, contending that agriculture is too important, and market failures too great, for developing country governments to take a *laissez-faire* approach towards the sector.

Case studies

There is a large body of literature covering these opposing views and related issues, which this study does not endeavour to examine. What this study does instead is to look very briefly at the experiences of six different countries, each of which stand out amongst developing countries as having enjoyed unusually high rates of economic growth and development. The chosen countries are:

- Indonesia
- South Korea
- Malaysia
- Viet Nam
- Chile
- Botswana.

Four of these countries are located in East Asia, where most of the economic success stories are concentrated. In Africa there have been very few examples of sustained economic growth, though Botswana is a notable exception. Chile is included because it stands out as one of Latin America's fastest-growing economies in recent decades.

The case studies illustrate government policy on agriculture and agricultural trade at the time when the economies of these countries were beginning to take off. They shed some light on whether agriculture and the associated policy environment at this time made a significant contribution, either to these countries' rapid economic growth, or to broader development goals such as poverty reduction and the equitable distribution of wealth. Answering this question may reveal the extent to which governments should retain their powers to intervene in trade as opposed to relinquishing them in favour of market liberalisation.

It is hoped that lessons might be extracted from these case studies for other developing countries, whose economies have as yet failed to take off. Relatively little attempt is made to evaluate more recent policy questions in the case study countries, especially in those countries that have been growing rapidly for many years and in which agriculture is now a much smaller component of the economy. The role of agriculture and, hence, the most appropriate policy environment in advanced developing countries are very different from those that applied in those same countries at an earlier stage of their development; and, indeed, they are very different from what is relevant to poorer developing countries today.

Each of the case studies tells a unique story and, although they share some common features in terms of structure and content, the emphasis in all of them is slightly different. In part, this reflects constraints in terms of what data and literature could be accessed within the available timeframe. It also reflects variations between countries in the focus of existing research and in the primary data that are actually available. Despite these constraints, the country studies do reveal very real differences in each country's experience. These differences are informative and add value to the lessons that might be learned.

Whilst the title of this study emphasises agricultural trade policy, it is necessary to stress at this point that agricultural trade policy and its effects cannot be examined in isolation from the wider policy environment of which it is a part. Intervention in trade is one of a number of instruments used by governments to meet their agricultural policy objectives. However, many policy instruments that do not relate directly to trade do, nevertheless, affect a country's international competitiveness and therefore have important implications for agricultural trade. Indeed, the WTO's agricultural negotiating agenda specifically addresses many of these instruments, in addition to those that affect trade directly, such as tariffs and other border controls. Thus, it is within the context of the broader agricultural policy environment that the objectives and outcomes of trade policy in the case studies are examined.

Finally, it should be noted that agricultural policy is itself part of a larger policy environment that includes macro-economic policy and government policy relating to other sectors of the economy. Whilst there is little scope for a detailed exploration of these wider policy areas in a study as short as this, they do need to be borne in mind, because their impact on agriculture is often as great as (if not greater than) the impact of agricultural policy *per se*.

Overview of country studies

This section provides a brief and comparative overview of the case study findings. Whilst the common characteristic of each of the six countries is that they have all experienced a stage of rapid and prolonged economic growth, some, such as South Korea, Malaysia, and Botswana, entered this stage before others, as can be seen from Table 1 below.

Table 1: Average annual per capita growth in GDP (%)

	1961–70	1971–80	1981–90	1991–2000
South Korea	5.6	5.5	7.4	5.1
Malaysia	3.5	5.3	3.1	4.5
Indonesia	1.8	5.4	4.4	2.7
Viet Nam	—	—	—	5.8
Chile	1.8	1.2	2.1	4.9
Botswana	5.6	11.1	7.1	1.9
East Asia & Pacific	2.4	4.6	5.6	6.4
Latin America & Caribbean	2.5	3.4	-0.9	1.6
South Asia	1.9	0.7	3.3	3.3
Sub-Saharan Africa	2.6	0.7	-1.1	-0.4
World	3.4	1.8	1.4	1.2

Source: author's calculations based upon World Bank Development Indicators, 2004 (GDP in constant 1995 US$)

Resource endowment

Another feature common to most of the countries in the study (except South Korea) is that they are relatively rich in natural resources. Malaysia has been the world's largest exporter of tin and rubber; Chile is the world's biggest producer of copper; and Botswana is the world's largest exporter of diamonds. Malaysia and Indonesia are both net exporters of oil, and Viet Nam is now the world's second largest exporter of rice. In some countries, especially Botswana, these resources have played a central role in economic growth and development. South Korea, by contrast, has fewer natural resources. To overcome this obstacle, the country harnessed its human resources and low labour costs to become one of the world's most successful export-oriented manufacturing economies. It embarked on this strategy in the early 1960s at a time when there was a growing demand in rich countries for cheap manufactured products and when there was little international competition from other low-cost producers.

The role of agriculture

Not surprisingly, agriculture played a very large role in the economies of all of the countries prior to take-off, as a source of both GDP and employment. The exception is Chile, which like much of Latin America achieved independence and began the process of urbanisation/industrialisation much earlier than other developing countries.

A common feature of agriculture in the Asian countries is the pivotal role of rice. It is the staple food in all four countries and dominates agricultural production in each – although in Malaysia a much larger proportion of agricultural land is devoted to export crops. Most rice production is carried out by relatively poor smallholders farming small parcels of land. The performance of the rice sector is therefore the main focus of policy-makers concerned with food security and poverty reduction. In Botswana, sorghum and maize play a similar role, and in Chile wheat is the dominant crop, although in Chile a large proportion of staple food production also takes place on large farms.

Agricultural export commodities have fulfilled an important function in the agricultural sectors of all countries, with the exception of Korea. Malaysia has long been a major exporter of rubber and palm oil; the growth of Chile's agricultural sector has been driven by the export of horticultural products; in Botswana beef exports have been the most successful part of the agricultural economy; Indonesia has long been an exporter of a variety of tropical agricultural commodities; and Viet Nam has recently become a major exporter of rice and an increasingly important exporter of other tropical products.

Agricultural policy environment

The agricultural policy environment before and during take-off can be examined in terms of its objectives regarding producers and consumers and in terms of the policy instruments used to achieve those objectives. Differences between countries and within countries over time are evident in relation to both.

Policy objectives in relation to consumers and producers

Through its impact on domestic prices, agricultural trade policy is one of a number of instruments that can be used to influence both the price that consumers pay for food and the income received by farmers. In applying trade and other price-related policies, a trade-off needs to be made between the welfare of producers on the one hand and of consumers on the other. The six countries have approached this dilemma in different ways.

At the early stages of its development, South Korea favoured consumers over producers. Cheap food imports kept rural incomes low, thereby stimulating rural–urban migration and enhancing the supply of cheap labour that was integral to the success of export-oriented industrialisation. The government subsequently reversed this policy, using the proceeds of industrial growth for agricultural investment, and raising import barriers to lift domestic agricultural prices.

In Malaysia and Indonesia, policies have been generally supportive of rice producers, who represent the most sizeable and politically influential socio-economic group in each of these countries. However, in Indonesia in particular, efforts have been made to achieve a balance between the interests of producers and consumers – neither has been especially favoured over the other. Both Malaysia and Indonesia are net importers of rice (although in the mid-1980s Indonesia did temporarily achieve food self-sufficiency). Control over imports has given governments in both countries considerable influence over domestic prices, allowing them to pursue domestic price stability which, as in other Asian countries, has been a priority concern (see discussion below).

In Viet Nam, a natural exporter of rice, producers were originally penalised by the government's trade policy, as export restraints depressed the domestic price of rice in the interests of consumers. These restraints have now been lifted, to the benefit of most Vietnamese farmers.

In Chile, before economic take-off, producers were implicitly taxed, despite the existence of agricultural import barriers. This implicit taxation arose largely as a result of agricultural export restraints and the bias towards the industrial sector, which reduced the ratio of agricultural prices to non-agricultural prices and kept a cap on domestic food prices. Economic growth in Chile coincided with the removal of this bias as internal and external trade were liberalised.

Botswana's approach was different again. As a net importer of food, Botswana kept domestic food prices under control by operating a liberal import regime. At the same time, revenues from diamond exports financed massive farm subsidies that helped to keep producer prices above their free-market level.

In each of the six countries the attitudes of policy makers towards producers and consumers reflect a number of different factors: the relative political influence of the two groups; concerns about poverty and equity; and the perceived importance of domestic agricultural production, both as a means of achieving greater food self-sufficiency and as a source of economic growth.

Agricultural producers in all of the six countries have benefited as a result of one or more of these factors. Table 2 identifies those factors that stand out as being particularly important in the individual case studies. The blank cells do not signify that the associated factor was unimportant, only that it might have been less important than others.

Table 2: Main factors leading to pro-agricultural policy

	Political influence of rural majority	Equity and poverty concerns	Food self-sufficiency goals	Agriculture explicit part of wider growth strategy
South Korea	x	x	x	
Malaysia	x	x	x	x
Indonesia	x	x	x	x
Viet Nam		x	x	x
Botswana		x	x	
Chile				x

Price stability

Price stability is a policy objective that deserves a special mention, particularly in relation to the Asian countries and rice. The world market for rice has traditionally been very 'thin' – that is, the volume of rice traded on the international market has tended to be small in relation to total production. A thin market leads to volatility, with relatively small changes in production having a relatively large effect on the size of traded surpluses and, hence, on world market prices. The 'thinness' of the international rice market partly explains the desire for rice self-sufficiency that has been an important feature of rice policy throughout much of East Asia. International price instability also explains the widespread use of trade restrictions to insulate domestic markets from this volatility. Without such intervention, consumers and producers (especially the poorer ones) would be very vulnerable to the peaks (consumers) and troughs (producers) of international price movements. It is worth noting, however, that the thinness and volatility of the international rice market is at least in part due to the combined effect of so many countries pursuing restrictive trade practices (Gulati and Narayanan 2002). Price stabilisation policies have also been pursued in Chile in relation to the main food staples.

Key policy instruments

A wide range of policy instruments has been used to achieve government objectives for producers and consumers prior to and during economic take-off. In the Asian food-importing countries, trade policy in relation to the staple food sector has been achieved through state trading monopolies (Malaysia and Indonesia) and through import licences and quotas (South Korea) – tariffs have played a minimal role. In the other food-importing nations, food was either permitted to enter the country tariff-free (Botswana) or was subject to a variable levy aimed at stabilising domestic prices (Chile). In the food-exporting nations (Viet Nam and Chile), trade policy during the take-off phase was largely characterised by the removal of export restrictions, although both countries had placed heavy restrictions on trade prior to that. In Botswana a state-owned marketing board monopolised beef exports, whereas in Malaysia exports were carried out by the private sector and were subject only to taxes.

Interventions in domestic markets have also played a role in achieving government price objectives. These interventions typically involved a state marketing board, which buys to defend a minimum support price for producers, and sells to prevent consumer prices from exceeding a government-stipulated ceiling. These boards have played an important role in all of the case study countries, except in Chile, which largely abandoned this practice when the economy was liberalised. Generally speaking, interventions to defend domestic prices require a degree of control over trade, to prevent domestic prices from aligning themselves with international ones. However, this may be less imperative in relation to producer support prices in remote rural areas, which are poorly integrated with urban and international markets and which rely heavily on government subsidies.

The other important set of policy instruments relates to subsidised inputs and credit combined with public sector investment in rural infrastructure and agricultural research and extension. This form of agricultural support has been a major feature of policy in all of the case study countries, but was particularly important in Asian countries where, from the mid-1960s onwards, the successful adoption of the new high-yielding rice varieties associated with the Green Revolution necessitated new skills on the part of farmers, combined with irrigation and a package of inputs that included seeds, fertilisers, and pesticides.

Agricultural performance

In the Asian countries, agriculture responded well to price incentives and to the public sector's active support for Green Revolution technologies. Rice output increased substantially, with major improvements in yield, higher cropping intensities (number of harvests per year), and new areas developed for irrigated rice production. The productivity improvements that resulted from the Green Revolution may have been much slower to emerge, had governments not created an environment in which the risks to farmers of adopting these new and initially unfamiliar technologies were greatly reduced. The price stability resulting from government intervention in trade and domestic markets gave farmers confidence that output prices would not collapse at harvest time. This, combined with input and credit subsidies, increased their incentives to invest in the new and more productive technologies.

In Botswana, by contrast, government support for staple food production has been far less successful. Output and yields have fallen despite massive government investment in the sector. However, government intervention in Botswana's beef sector has been more effective and the Botswana Meat Commission, which holds the statutory monopoly on beef exports, has generally been regarded as one of Africa's more efficient state marketing boards. In Chile agricultural performance has also improved greatly in response to government policies, although there, unlike in the Asian countries, the main policy thrust has been towards market liberalisation and the privatisation of agricultural services.

Agriculture and economic growth

The relationship between agricultural performance and economic growth is a complex one. Agriculture's direct contribution to GDP growth comes from growth in agricultural value added. The latter is a function of physical output and the unit value of output net of input costs. Since agricultural value added has generally grown in all of the countries concerned, except in Botswana during the 1990s (World Bank 2005), agriculture can, in this sense, be said to have made a contribution to their GDP growth.

Agricultural growth as a catalyst for growth outside the agricultural sector

However, the picture is more complicated than that. First, resources used in agriculture are resources that are not being used to add value in other parts of the economy. In Korea, for example, some models suggest that the economy would have grown more quickly had policies from the 1970s onwards (especially trade policies) not induced a transfer of resources to the agricultural sector from other, more productive sectors of the economy (Diao et al. 2002).

Second, agriculture can also contribute to growth through its catalytic effects upon growth in other sectors of the economy. In Asia it has been estimated that a one dollar increase in agricultural income also increases the income accruing to local enterprises by 80 cents (Gulati and Narayanan 2002). Growth in agricultural productivity is fundamental to this process through a combination of the following effects (or 'growth linkages'):

- It allows resources (land, labour, and capital) to be released from agricultural production to aid the expansion of other sectors, such as manufacturing and services. This transfer of resources out of agriculture can take place either through farmers investing their surplus time and resources in non-agricultural enterprises, or through governments taxing agricultural income and investing the proceeds outside the agricultural sector.

- If greater productivity leads to a greater volume of output it will increase the demand for (and hence growth in) the sectors that provide farm inputs and services and perform post-harvest processing and marketing activities.

- Greater productivity may translate into higher farm incomes, thus allowing farmers to increase their demand for non-agricultural goods and services as consumers. One of the reasons why the import-substitution industrialisation policies of many developing countries have failed in the past is because they gave insufficient attention to rural incomes. The result was that the market for the output of domestic industries was very limited because the majority of the population lived in rural areas. Korea overcame this problem by developing an export-oriented industrial policy. Indonesia, Malaysia, and Viet Nam have all done the same, whilst also recognising the importance of rural growth and development.

- Finally, increased agricultural productivity can lead to lower food prices. Not only does this help to increase food security and reduce poverty but, by increasing the real incomes of consumers, it creates additional demand for non-agricultural goods and services.

Whether or not improved agricultural productivity does lead to growth in other sectors of the economy depends of course on whether the institutional environment is conducive for other sectors to grow – allowing the urban and rural economies to make efficient use of the resources released from agriculture and enabling them to meet the additional demand generated by agricultural growth. In contrast with other developing countries, most of the case studies, especially the Asian ones, stand out as possessing such an environment, which includes, amongst other characteristics, political and macro-economic stability, effective government, and good levels of basic education (World Bank 1993).

However, these conditions alone do not ensure that economic growth results from improved agricultural productivity – for agriculture's impact upon growth depends upon how the productivity improvements are achieved in the first place. For example, if they arise as a result of policies that transfer resources away from other, more productive sectors of the economy, then their net contribution to wider economic growth can be diminished.

Agricultural productivity growth in Korea (which has been substantial) and in Botswana (where it has been less substantial) appears to fit this latter model, and it is hard to conclude that improved agricultural productivity or the policies that helped bring it about have contributed significantly to economic take-off in these countries. In Korea, agricultural productivity only began to rise once manufacturing-led growth was already well under way and generating resources that could be used to lift the agricultural sector out of stagnation. Indeed, it was initially stagnant (rather than improving) agricultural productivity that drove resources out of agriculture and into the growing industrial sector – it was labour, rather than capital, that was the main resource to make this move, since there was little surplus capital in the rural areas at this time. In Botswana, what improvements there have been in agricultural productivity have been driven largely by growth in other sectors of the economy (notably the diamond sector), rather than themselves being the driving force behind that growth.

However, if one looks to Indonesia, Malaysia, Viet Nam, and Chile one sees a rather different picture. For these countries it is easier to argue that large strides in agricultural productivity, and the policies that helped to achieve them, have made a significant contribution to wider economic growth. In contrast with Korea and Botswana, productivity improvements do not appear to have depended upon large transfers from an already rapidly expanding non-agricultural sector.

Price stabilisation and economic growth

It also worth mentioning once again the policy of price stabilisation, since a stable price environment, especially in relation to food prices, has been identified as making a significant contribution to growth. One of the main objectives of agricultural policy interventions in the Asian economies reviewed in this study has been the stabilisation of rice prices. Rice plays an extremely important role in the region owing to its large contribution to agricultural value added, food security, total calorie consumption, and the incomes of small producers. Dawe (2001) sets out the case for the stabilisation of rice prices in Asia. The case is based upon the benefits of price stability for producers and consumers, as well as its macro-economic benefits.

Because a high proportion of consumer expenditure in Asian countries (especially amongst the poor) is devoted to rice, changes in the price of rice can have a significant impact on consumers' real incomes. Sharply rising prices lead either to a reduction in calorie consumption or to a diversion of expenditure away from other essential nutrients (such as proteins, fats, and vitamins) and other basic needs. Price stabilisation helps to eliminate the crises that poor people often experience under these circumstances and the harmful long-term effects of these crises. Price stability also benefits producers by protecting them from the harmful effects that collapsing prices can have on their incomes and, hence, on their consumption. Whilst producers may forgo the benefits of rising prices, and consumers may miss out on the benefits of falling prices, these benefits are likely to be outweighed by the benefits of avoiding the crises that are associated with large price swings: the marginal benefits of consumption tend to increase as consumption falls, especially when it falls towards or below the poverty line.

Instability in the price of a basic food commodity, such as rice, can also affect macro-economic growth and stability. When demand for a food commodity is not very responsive to prices changes (which it often is not), and when a high proportion of total expenditure is devoted to that commodity (as is typically the case in poor countries), those price changes will affect demand in other sectors of the economy, owing to their effect on the real incomes of consumers. This can be economically destabilising and harmful to growth and investment in the wider economy. Stabilisation policies can therefore contribute positively to economic growth. According to Timmer (2000), rice price stabilisation in Indonesia added between half and one per cent to the country's annual GDP growth rate during the 1970s.

Dawe (2001) asserts that free trade is likely to lead to greater instability in the domestic prices of rice for Asian producers and consumers. Although the liberalisation of the world rice market would reduce volatility in the world price of rice it would not, according to Dawe, deliver the same level of price stability that has been achieved under the government-led price stabilisation schemes that have existed in Indonesia, Malaysia, Korea, and other countries in the region.

Social stability

Finally in this section, it is important to note the relationship between economic growth and social stability. In all of the case study countries, governments appear to have been very aware of the potentially destabilising effects of disaffection on the part of a large and impoverished section of society. Government support for smallholders combined with food price stabilisation policies have helped to maintain social stability in a rapidly changing world. These interventions, which in many cases involve government control over international trade, have reduced the threats to growth posed by the sorts of social unrest that many of these countries witnessed in the years before their economies took off.

Distributional impact of agricultural policies

Producers

In the Asian countries and in Botswana, relatively poor smallholders are responsible for most staple food production. These producers have benefited from government support for the sector, although in Viet Nam these benefits were only fully realised when the government removed restrictions on rice exports. In a number of countries (Korea, Malaysia, and Botswana) there is very clear evidence of governments using the instruments of agricultural policy in an attempt to transfer resources from more prosperous parts of the economy to vulnerable groups in the rural sector (i.e. smallholders in the staple food sector). In Chile the situation is rather different. Large farms play a much bigger role in agricultural production than is the case in the other countries in the study. Consequently much of the direct (and sizeable) benefits of agricultural liberalisation and export expansion have accrued to such farmers, largely bypassing rural smallholders, who typically occupy marginal land and do not produce a marketable surplus.

Agricultural support policies, especially where they promote modern, input-intensive technologies, are always vulnerable to the criticism that they by-pass resource-poor farmers who are either too poor to afford modern inputs, have too little land to produce a marketable surplus, or who live in remote areas that are unsuited to modern technologies or are beyond the reach of government support services. To a certain extent this is a valid criticism in all of the case study countries. Nevertheless, a very large proportion of the beneficiaries of agricultural support (notably in East Asia) have been poor farmers with the good fortune to live in areas suited to Green Revolution technologies and in which it was possible both to access affordable (subsidised) inputs, and to sell crops at a minimum guaranteed price.

The landless poor

Support for agricultural producers also benefits the wider rural economy for reasons mentioned earlier – by releasing resources for investment in non-agricultural activities and generating additional demand for goods and services produced outside the farm sector. These rural 'growth linkages' generate employment for the landless poor and help to raise their incomes. In Chile, where land ownership is highly skewed, this is probably the main way in which the rural poor have benefited from agricultural growth. In the Asian countries, where smallholders play a much larger role in production, the rural growth linkages may be even stronger, since smallholders tend to spend a larger proportion of their income and invest a larger proportion of their surpluses within the local rural economy than is the case with large farmers.

Consumers

The impact of government policy on consumers has been varied. In Asia, the adoption of Green Revolution technologies, for which governments have provided considerable support, reduced the costs of food production, making food cheaper in real terms than it would otherwise have been. This is a clear benefit to consumers throughout the region, especially the poor who spend a large proportion of their incomes on food. Poor consumers have also benefited from price stabilisation policies (as discussed above).

In Indonesia, government interventions in trade and pricing sought to balance the interests of producers and consumers, favouring neither one group nor the other over the longer term. In Viet Nam, government trade policy initially sought to protect consumers from the higher prices that would exist under a more liberal trade regime. However, the recent reversal of this policy means that consumers now pay more for rice than they might otherwise have done. In Korea and Malaysia, consumers have generally paid more for their food than they would have done under a more liberal trading regime (especially in Korea), and this has made poor consumers more vulnerable. In Botswana trade policy does not appear to have greatly penalised consumers, and in Chile trade controls have been used to maintain a ceiling price on important food staples.

There will always be winners and losers as a result of economic change and the policies that help to shape it. What most of the case study countries appear to have achieved is a degree of balance between the various major interest groups in society. The instruments of trade and fiscal policy have been used to promote growth and also in many cases to compensate groups who are more vulnerable to rapid economic change.

Lessons for other developing countries

What lessons do the experiences of the case study countries provide for other developing countries, especially those that are still growing very slowly? Could today's less-developed countries also achieve economic success by pursuing the same sorts of policies as were pursued in the case study countries, especially in relation to agriculture and agricultural trade? Needless to say, there are no simple answers to this question. Economic growth in the case study countries has benefited from a number of circumstances that may not be easy to replicate in other countries.

Good endowments of natural resources (mineral, agricultural, or both) have favoured all but Korea, which benefited instead from being one of the first developing countries to specialise in cheap manufactured exports. Nevertheless, many less successful developing countries are also rich in natural resources, but have simply failed to harness them effectively.

However, there are other important differences between some of the case study countries and other, less-developed countries. The dominant position of rice in the Asian countries, and the availability of modern high-yielding varieties suited to the growing conditions in much of the region, have arguably made it easier to design and implement effective agricultural policies than might be the case in countries where patterns of consumption and production are more diverse, and where the physical environment is more hostile. The conditions in Africa, for example, are very different from those prevailing in East and South-East Asia. Apart from the more hostile physical environment in Africa, the commodities that dominate rural production systems – maize, sorghum, millet, plantains, and root crops – are much more varied. Moreover, they are not always the same as those consumed by urban consumers, who increasingly favour imported food grains such as wheat and rice.

Nevertheless, the price of one staple food does affect the price of others, so it is potentially possible to influence producer prices by policies targeted at a few key commodities, such as maize, wheat, or rice, if there is the political will to do so. However, the linkages between the rural and urban sectors in Africa are often very weak, and the disparity between the politically influential urban population and the relatively weak rural majority is arguably greater than in the Asian countries reviewed in this study.

These differences in political economy, as well as in the physical environment, probably make it harder to apply policies in Africa that support agricultural producers and raise agricultural productivity than has been the case in much of East and South-East Asia (Timmer 2002a). That does not mean it is impossible. In parts of Eastern and Southern Africa, for instance, maize plays a particularly important role in rural patterns of production and consumption and, like rice in Asia, has often been a focus of government policies aimed at stimulating rural and agricultural growth. Unfortunately many past policies aimed at supporting staple food production have failed, because of a combination of financial constraints, corruption, and mismanagement. Moreover, in countries which have attempted to protect and subsidise producers while at the same time keeping food prices low, the resulting subsidies have led to unsustainable budget deficits and macro-economic instability, and have culminated in the structural adjustment and market liberalisation policies promoted and supported by the IMF and the World Bank.

The policies pursued by a number of the case study countries (Indonesia, Malaysia, and Korea) during economic take-off are clearly not consistent with the trade liberalisation agenda currently being promoted by the WTO and the international financial institutions. The WTO's Uruguay Round Agreement on Agriculture (URAA) gave 'special treatment' to rice in certain East Asian countries. This 'special treatment' permitted the continued use of non-tariff barriers to trade, such as state trading monopolies, variable import tariffs, and quotas (Healy et al. 1998; Dawe 2001). For other commodities and in other parts of the world there has been a shift away from non-tariff barriers (NTBs) to trade towards the use of tariffs as the main instrument for controlling imports. In many countries this shift took place initially as part of donor-financed structural adjustment programmes. However, the results of this process were subsequently locked into the trade liberalisation commitments that individual countries made within the URAA – commitments that prohibited the use of NTBs and set tariff ceilings and tariff reduction targets.

The URAA required that NTBs be converted into a tariff equivalent, which then acted as a ceiling for future tariffs. In the years following the agreement (six years in the case of developed countries and ten in the case of developing countries), countries were required to reduce these tariffs by an average of 36 per cent in the case of developed countries and 24 per cent in the case of developing countries, with a minimum reduction of 15 per cent per tariff line in developed countries and 10 per cent in developing countries. Least developed countries (LDCs) were not required to make reduction commitments.

The current Doha Round of negotiations is still under way, and it remains unclear what sort of agreement will be reached. Further 'substantial' liberalisation of agricultural trade (beyond what was achieved in the Uruguay Round) is high on the agenda, as is 'special and differential treatment' for developing countries. The agricultural negotiations are focused mainly on increasing market access, reducing export subsidies, and reducing other forms of domestic support (such as subsidies etc.). Market access commitments are likely to have the most immediate impact on agricultural policy in developing countries, because of the relatively small role played by export subsidies and other forms of domestic support in these countries.

Market access involves further reductions in bound tariffs (the ceilings that were set in the Uruguay Round) and increases in the access that exists via tariff rate quotas (TRQs: import quotas that are allowed access at a reduced tariff level). As in the Uruguay Round, special and differential treatment for developing countries is likely to translate into less demanding tariff reduction and TRQ commitments and longer implementation periods, although precise numbers have yet to be agreed upon. LDCs apparently will not have to make reduction commitments, although some of these may argue for increases (rather than reductions) in the level at which certain tariffs were bound in the URAA.

Clearly, tariffs have become and will in the future remain a much more important trade policy instrument than they were in the past. Can they be used to control domestic prices and incentives as effectively as NTBs? In theory, yes, providing they can be varied across a wide enough range at relatively short notice – i.e. in the case of import tariffs, raised to a sufficiently high level to protect a domestic floor price when domestic prices are falling. How is the Doha Round likely to affect this 'policy space'? This depends, first, upon how it deals with the issue of varying tariffs/duties, and second, on the level at which tariff ceilings are bound. 'Variable import levies' were treated by the Uruguay Round as a form of NTB and were therefore prohibited. Yet the precise legal definition of a variable import levy remains unclear and has been the subject of trade disputes. Some argue that a variable duty/tariff is permissible providing it does not exceed the upper bound tariff levels committed to under the URAA – others disagree. A Doha deal could possibly provide greater clarity on the subject.

Currently, it seems as if countries will be allowed to designate certain commodities as 'sensitive' (for developed countries) or 'special' (for developing countries). Added flexibility in the use of tariffs will be permitted for these products. The URAA includes provisions ('Special Safeguards') that allow additional tariffs to be applied, according to a clearly defined formula, in the event of domestic prices falling below a critical threshold. In the Doha Round, the number of commodities that can be designated as 'sensitive'/'special' and the way that they are to be treated is clearly an important negotiating issue.

In conclusion, developing countries today face a very different international policy environment to that which existed when the economies of the countries in this study were beginning to take off. The flexibility of policy-makers in relation to trade policy is much more limited than it was 30 or 40 years ago. Smallholder development strategies of the sort pursued by the East Asian case study countries were underpinned by government use of trade policy instruments to influence domestic prices (protecting floor prices for farmers as well as ceiling prices for consumers). If less-developed countries today are to pursue similar strategies, they need to have a reasonable amount of flexibility in their use of duties and tariffs, since the much wider range of instruments that were available to governments prior to the Uruguay Round are no longer available.

The current liberalising agenda provides a fair amount of support for the sorts of strategies pursued by Chile, Botswana and, more recently, Viet Nam. However, developing countries wishing to follow the agricultural development strategies that were pursued by Korea, Malaysia, and Indonesia in previous decades may need more policy space than the current liberalising agenda would naturally wish to concede.

Indonesia

Economic growth and development

The Indonesian economy began to take off in the 1970s. Average growth rates in the 1960s were relatively low as a result of macro-economic instability and political upheavals that caused severe disruption mid-way through the decade. However, average per capita growth rates in the 1970s and 1980s were comparable with the fastest-growing economies in the region, as the country shifted from a relatively inward-looking approach to a more outward, export-oriented approach to economic development.

The role of agriculture in the economy

In 1960 over 50 per cent of Indonesia's GDP came from the agricultural sector and, whilst this figure had fallen to just 17 per cent by 2003, agriculture's contribution is still higher than for other countries in the sample, with the exception of Viet Nam. The proportion of the population employed in agriculture fell below 50 per cent in the early 1990s, but standing at 44 per cent in 2001, it is still very high compared with other countries. In the early 1960s the contribution of agricultural raw materials to total merchandise exports (over 45 per cent in 1962) was also higher than for other countries, except Malaysia. By 2000 agricultural raw materials represented only about 3.5 per cent of total exports, but this was still higher than the regional average of about 2 per cent. Food exports have been around 10 per cent of total exports since the early 1990s, having fallen from around 20 per cent in the 1960s and early 1970s.

This case study focuses on Indonesia's rice policy. As elsewhere in the region, rice is the staple food commodity and consistently contributes about 50 per cent of the population's total calorie consumption (FAO 2004). As a major component of agricultural value added, it also contributed significantly to GDP in the early years of Indonesia's development, although this contribution has fallen as the economy has diversified away from agriculture. In 1967 in Jakarta rice accounted for about 31 per cent of the cost of living: its price therefore had an important influence on other sectors of the economy, owing to its effect on real incomes and its role as a 'wage good'.

Rice – policy and trade

Rice has always been the main focus of Indonesia's policy on agriculture and food security, and the most consistent thread running through this policy has been the government's endeavours to stabilise the price of rice. The latter objective has also been at the centre of policy governing the external trade in rice.

The role of BULOG in domestic and international trade

Price stability has been pursued by intervening in the market to defend a nationwide ceiling price for consumers and a floor price for producers. Since 1967 this policy has been implemented by BULOG, the government-controlled Food Logistics Agency (in conjunction with regional DOLOGs). The policy instruments used by BULOG to achieve this are summarised in Box 1.

Box 1: Instruments for stabilising Indonesian rice prices

BULOG defended a floor price and a ceiling price through a combination of the following policy instruments:

monopoly control over international trade in rice

access to an unlimited line of credit (at heavily subsidised interest rates in the early years; at commercial rates with a Bank of Indonesia guarantee in later years)

procurement of as much rice as necessary by DOLOGs to lift the price in rural markets to the policy-determined floor price

extensive logistical facilities, including a nationwide complex of warehouses, which permitted seasonal storage of substantial quantities of rice (including the one million tonnes for the 'iron stock' that was considered essential for Indonesia's food security)

These rice stocks, accumulated through domestic procurement in defence of the floor price and, when these supplies were inadequate, through imports, were then used to defend a ceiling price in urban markets.

Source: Timmer 2002b

An important feature of government intervention in Indonesia's rice sector lay in its relationship with the private sector. Unlike in many developing countries, the policy sought to encourage private sector involvement in domestic trade rather than replace it. In a normal year, less than 10 per cent of annual rice production would be handled by BULOG (Ellis 1993) – more than 90 per cent was handled by the private sector. The margin between the floor price and the ceiling price was set so as to allow private traders to operate profitably within it, providing they were efficient. Stable prices were considered beneficial to traders as well as to producers and consumers.

Another important characteristic of the government's intervention in the rice sector was that, although domestic prices were not linked to world prices in the short term – BULOG's monopoly over international trade ensured that short-term shocks on the international market were not transmitted to the domestic market – they did follow long-term trends in world prices. Pricing policy was relatively neutral in relation to welfare transfers between producers and consumers (Siamwalla 2001). When world prices were low, producers were protected from cheap imports, but when world prices were high, producers were implicitly taxed in order to maintain the ceiling price for consumers. This contrasts with the experience of many other developing countries, where price interventions have often subsidised one group at the expense of the other.

BULOG was established at a time of enormous political and economic upheaval (Timmer 2002a). From the late 1950s onwards, Indonesia's economy slid towards deepening crisis, as budget deficits widened, inflation spiralled out of control, and foreign exchange became increasingly scarce. By 1966 yields and per capita consumption of rice were lower than they had been in 1958. This economic instability coincided with severe political unrest, which in 1966 eventually ended the rule of President Sukarno and ushered in Suharto's 'New Order' regime. The new government viewed the revival of rice production and, in particular, the stabilisation of rice prices as essential to the restoration of political and economic stability. BULOG was created to achieve this and was also charged with providing monthly rations of rice to the military and to the civil service.

From 1970 efforts to revive rice production included fertiliser and farm credit subsidies, as well as the BULOG-supported floor price. In the mid-1970s the goal of self-sufficiency in rice production became a central feature of government policy. At the time Indonesia was importing large quantities of rice in order to meet domestic demand. A crisis in the world market in the early 1970s helped to motivate the drive towards self-sufficiency. Adverse weather conditions throughout much of Asia pushed up world prices, and by

1973 it became extremely difficult to purchase rice on international markets. The crisis highlighted Indonesia's vulnerability to dependence on what has historically been a very thin global market. As a consequence, domestic production gained increasing attention from policy makers.

Performance

Indonesia's policies in the 1970s and 1980s appear to have been very successful on a number of counts, including their effects on rice production, price stability, and food self-sufficiency. The period between 1975 and 1996 was a period of considerable price stability and BULOG's success in defending the floor price was widely cited as a key factor in the unprecedented increase in rice production (Timmer 2002a). BULOG's success in the rice sector led to it also being given responsibility for other commodities, including wheat, corn, soybeans, and sugar.

In contrast with similar agencies in many other developing countries, BULOG appears to have been relatively immune to the problems of corruption, at least until the mid-1990s. Siamwalla (2001) attributes this to Indonesia's uniquely powerful presidency and to the president's personal commitment to the success of BULOG and its objectives. According to Siamwalla, this commitment was probably linked to the president's awareness that, without stability in the rice market, his own political power might be threatened.

Production and food self-sufficiency

Before 1968 the average rice yield stood at about 1.7 metric tonnes (mt) per hectare. In 1968 it increased to 2.1 mt/ha and continued upwards in the following years. Table 3 shows the dramatic growth in output and yields during the 1970s and 1980s. The average annual output in the 1970s was 63 per cent higher than in the previous decade, and grew by a further 67 per cent in the 1980s. Much of this increase came from rising yields, which increased by an average of 43 per cent and 44 per cent respectively over the same periods, as well as from greater cropping intensity (the number of harvests per year), which is reflected in growth in the total harvested area.

Table 3: Indonesian rice production

Average annual production indicators	1961–70	1971–80	1981–90	1991–2000
Area (1,000 ha)	7,455	8,510	9,828	11,277
Output (1,000 mt)	14,335	23,424	39,022	48,997
Yield (mt/ha)	1.9	2.8	4.0	4.3
% growth in relation to previous decade				
Area		14	15	15
Output		63	67	26
Yield		43	44	9

Source: FAO 2004

Although increases in productivity were closely linked to the new Green Revolution technologies that were emerging in Asia at the time, output price stability and input subsidies gave Indonesian farmers the confidence and incentive to invest in the new technologies. Between 1976 and 1983 the fertiliser subsidy was gradually increased, by maintaining a constant nominal price for fertiliser whilst the floor price for rice rose in line with inflation. Other contributions to increasing production during this period included the 1978 currency devaluation and expanding oil revenues (due to the 1970s oil price hikes) which helped to finance public sector investment in agriculture, including investment in rural infrastructure, such as irrigation systems, roads, and market centres.

By 1984 Indonesia had become self-sufficient in rice and remained so for about a decade (see Figure 1). Once achieved, self-sufficiency in rice production was strictly enforced. This put financial pressure on BULOG, since its price stabilisation activities now had to focus on interventions in the domestic market, rather than simply varying the level of imports. It required additional investment in transport, processing, and marketing infrastructure, and lengthened storage times, adding to the financial burden of the operation as well as to its complexity.

Figure 1: Indonesia – net imports of rice

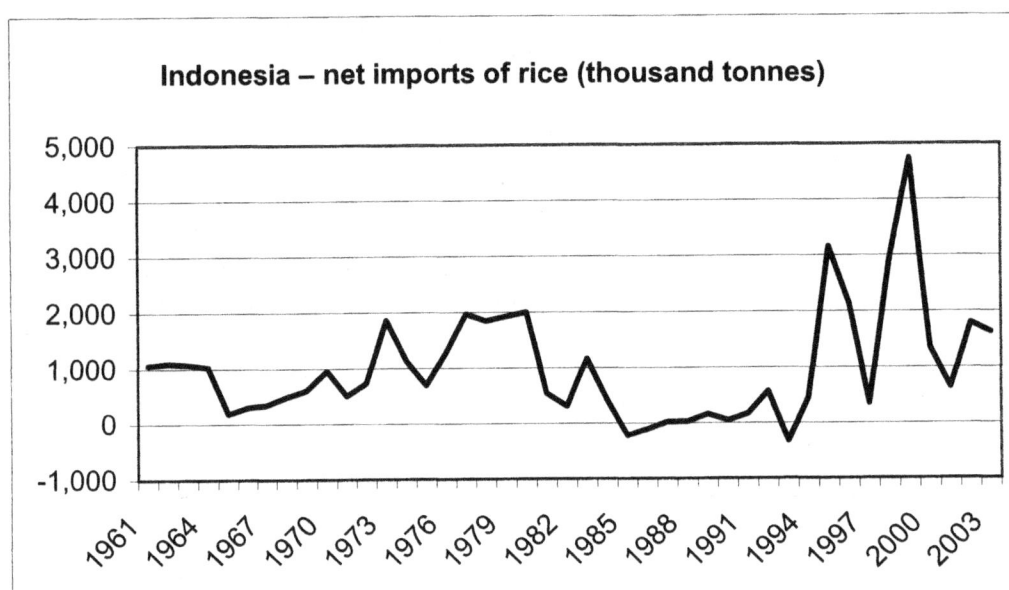

Source: based on data from FAO 2004

Additionally, the surpluses that BULOG accumulated in defending the floor price could only be disposed of on the international market at very low prices. Ironically, prices were low, in large part, because of BULOG's success in boosting Indonesia's output of rice – the country was traditionally one of the world's major rice importers. According to Timmer (2002a), 'BULOG's outstanding credits from the Central Bank became a significant proportion of total bank credit for the whole economy. The agency became a significant macroeconomic actor'. The financial pressures forced BULOG gradually to reduce producer price incentives, and the rapid growth in rice production began to slow in the second half of the 1980s.

The impact of price stabilisation on economic growth

Econometric analysis examining the relationship between Indonesia's price stabilisation policies and economic growth points to a positive relationship between the two, especially in the early years of the policy (Dawe 1995). A summary of the results (Timmer 2002a) is presented in Box 2.

Box 2: Quantifying the economic benefits of rice price stabilisation in Indonesia

The contribution of BULOG's rice price stabilization activities in the early years of the New Order regime was very large ... from 1969 to 1974, the rice price stabilization program alone generated nearly 1 percentage point of economic growth each year, which was more than one-sixth of the total increase in output during that period. In the second Five-Year Plan, from 1974 to 1979, the contribution was 0.61 per cent per year, or 13.5 per cent of the total growth in per capita income ...

These estimates are probably lower bounds, because they do not credit the rice price stabilization program with any benefits from enhanced political stability and the greater confidence felt by investors because of such stability. These estimates also do not include the direct contribution of rice price stabilization to reduced variance in the rate of inflation, which also has a negative impact on economic growth (Barro and Sala-i-Martin, 1994; Dawe, 1996) ...

However, the benefits from stabilizing rice prices fell markedly over time. By the end of the fifth Five-Year Plan in 1994, stabilization activities contributed only 0.19 percentage points a year to economic growth, just 3.8 per cent of the total increase in per capita income during that period ...

The decline in benefits from stabilizing rice prices occurred because the share of rice in the economy fell over time, and this decline reduced the importance of spillovers from rice into other sectors of the economy. The impact of rice price stabilization on investment and economic growth thus declines at higher levels of per capita income (Timmer, 1989a, 1996c; Dawe,1995).

Source: Timmer 2002a

Impact on poverty

The direct impact of Indonesia's rice policy on poverty is determined by its effect on the poor, both as producers and as consumers. A large proportion of Indonesia's poor are small-scale rice farmers, and indeed most rice production is carried out by smallholders. This group has undoubtedly benefited greatly from government support for the sector, both in terms of price stabilisation and in terms of public sector investment in rural infrastructure and agricultural inputs. However, this support has not been at the expense of poor rice consumers, who have also benefited from the government's ceiling on rice prices. Moreover, policy-induced agricultural growth also contributes to growth in other sectors of the rural economy, thus providing employment opportunities for the landless poor.

The link between agricultural policy and macro-economic growth has already been noted above. According to Timmer (2002a), the reduction of poverty in the rural areas during the 1970s and 1980s helped to foster a climate in which the wider economy could develop and grow. This in turn provided further opportunities for poverty reduction. At a national level, poverty rates in the 1960s were much higher than they are today, despite the temporary setback resulting from the Asian financial crisis. In 1976 the incidence of absolute poverty stood at 40 per cent of the population, but by 1996 this figure had declined to just 12 per cent (Islam 2003). A different dataset provided by the World Bank (2005) suggests that by 2002 less than 8 per cent of the population were below the dollar-a-day poverty line, compared with 28 per cent in 1987.

Pressures for change

As the economy has grown and the macro-economic benefits of rice price stabilisation have diminished, the costs of stabilising prices have tended to rise. This has led to pressures for a more market-oriented policy and to a reconsideration of BULOG's role and ways in which its costs could be controlled. Measures that have been taken have included reducing the agency's role in distributing rice to the civil service and to the military; increasing operational efficiency; and reducing the emphasis on strict year-to-year self-sufficiency in rice production. In the early 1990s BULOG was once again allowed to stabilise prices by importing rice. This proved effective and, according to Timmer (2002a), 'contributed significantly to a more efficient and a more effective BULOG'.

However, in the latter half of the 1990s Indonesia entered a period of crisis. Severe drought and the Asian financial crisis contributed to major upheaval in the country's political and economic institutions. BULOG was not immune to these changes or to pressure from donors to liberalise. The agency's vulnerability to corruption appears to have increased in the mid-1990s (IFPP 2002), providing fuel for those seeking to diminish its powers. At the end of the 1990s, its monopoly over international trade in rice and its mandate to stabilise prices were removed. By 1999 the private sector was responsible for over half of Indonesia's total rice imports. The future role of BULOG and indeed the direction of rice policy as a whole remain uncertain.

The relative efficiency with which BULOG carried out its operations in the past and the positive influence of government intervention in the rice sector at a critical period of the country's growth are generally acknowledged (Timmer 2002a; Dawe 2001). However, it remains open to debate whether the policies of the past are the appropriate ones for the future.

South Korea

Economic growth and development

South Korea is the most advanced economy in the sample. It is a member of the OECD and during its development 'recorded the highest sustained level of economic growth ever achieved' (OECD 1999). In the 1950s, following the Korean War, income per capita was one of the lowest in the region, but since 1960 this has risen in real terms by a factor of more than ten. Growth, which had been relatively slow during the 1950s (OECD 1999), took off in the 1960s, averaging over 8 per cent per annum during that decade (5.6 per cent in per capita terms). High growth rates have been sustained in every subsequent decade.

The role of agriculture in the economy

Agriculture's role in the South Korean economy is now relatively small, as one would expect in an industrialised economy. In 2001 the sector represented 4 per cent of GDP and 10 per cent of employment. At the end of the Second World War the situation was very different, with 80 per cent of the labour force engaged in agriculture (Byun et al. 1975) and the sector accounting for 50 per cent of GDP (OECD 1999). South Korea was, and remains, one of the most densely populated countries in the world, with abundant labour but a relatively low per capita endowment of agricultural land. Land reforms implemented in the 1950s led to an equal distribution of land, compared with the situation in most other Asian countries. They also resulted in average farm sizes of less than one hectare (OECD 1999).

Owing to the limitations of its natural resource base, South Korea has never been a natural exporter of agricultural commodities. In 2001, agricultural raw materials and food exports accounted for 1 per cent and 1.7 per cent respectively of merchandise exports. Although agriculture's contribution to exports in the 1960s was significantly higher (about 10 per cent in the case of agricultural raw materials and around 20 per cent for food exports), it was still quite low compared with many other countries in East Asia.

The government's policy on agricultural trade and its implications for poverty and economic growth are best understood by looking at the staple food sector. It is here that government interventions in domestic and international trade are most significant. As elsewhere in the region, rice is the staple food and has played an important role in the country's development. 'Grains, particularly rice, were central to Korean economic life in the 1950s, and because of the importance of food in household budgets, grain price policy was an adjunct to monetary policy. The price of rice was a principal determinant of inflation and thus real urban wages' (Diao et al 2002).

Agricultural policy instruments

Interventions in agricultural trade have played a prominent role in the government's policy towards the sector. In the case of some commodities, notably rice and barley, direct government interventions in the domestic market have also played a major part:

- Import licences and quotas have historically been the main instruments for controlling trade and domestic prices. For many commodities (especially rice) these have at times led to a virtual ban on imports. Tariffs have had a relatively minor influence on trade flows.

- The most significant interventions in the domestic market involve government procurement of grain from farmers and sales to consumers (especially the military and public sector workers). The government buying and selling prices have varied in accordance with policy objectives. The same can be said for the volume of government grain transactions, which in the case of rice increased from about 10 per cent of the market in the 1950s to 20–25 per cent in the 1960s, reaching 35–40 per cent by the early 1980s (Moon and Kang 1991).

- The government has also exerted control over the marketing of fertiliser, monopolising distribution and setting prices, especially during the 1960s and 1970s. Fertiliser subsidies have played a major role in efforts to raise agricultural yields.

In relation to farm output, the state-owned Agriculture and Fisheries Marketing Corporation (AFMC) was the main body responsible for achieving the government's price targets and implementing policy on international trade and domestic marketing.

Agricultural policy phases

Korea's agricultural trade policy has been associated with a number of different objectives, including producer and consumer welfare, food self-sufficiency, and price stability. Following Moon and Kang (1991) and Diao et al. (2002) it is possible to identify three distinct phases in the country's agricultural policy, each reflecting a different ordering of priorities. Food price stability has remained an important priority throughout, but the relative weights attached to producer and consumer welfare have shifted over time.

1950–1969

During the first phase, between 1950 and 1969, the government paid relatively little attention to the agricultural sector, since most of its attention was focused on promoting rapid industrialisation. During the 1960s Korea's industrial growth strategy, which until that time had focused mainly on import substitution, became more export-oriented, thus paving the way for the country's rapid economic growth. Low and stable consumer food prices were a key part of this strategy, as they made it easier to control nominal wages in the industrial sector and thereby increased the country's international competitiveness in the export of labour-intensive goods. In the mid-1960s food expenditure represented almost 60 per cent of living costs for the average urban worker (Moon and Kang 1991).

The instruments of agricultural policy (see above) were used to hold the price of food down. The process was assisted by large quantities of grain imported under the USA's food aid programme, which between 1956 and 1965 amounted to between 8 and 12 per cent of Korea's annual production (Moon and Kang 1991). Korean farmers were the main losers under this policy: low prices reduced their incomes and their incentives to produce. However, the resulting disparities between rural and urban incomes led to large-scale rural–urban migration during the 1960s, thus providing the labour force required for industrial expansion (Byun et al. 1975).

1970–1975

In 1969 policy-makers shifted their attention towards raising the welfare of farmers and reducing rural poverty. The government raised the price received by producers, whilst at the same time endeavouring to keep consumer prices low. In the rice sector, the average effective protection rate1 for producers rose from minus 26 per cent during 1962–69 to plus 39 per cent during 1970–79 (Moon and Kang 1991).

While rural migration played an important role in industrial growth, the influx of rural poor into the cities became increasingly hard to absorb and strengthened the case for greater government effort in the rural sector. The government's renewed focus on rural development involved massive investment in rural infrastructure. This was facilitated through the Saemaul (New Community) movement, an initiative to encourage collective action by farmers in the development of rural infrastructure and farm services.

Increased support for the rural sector during this period also reflected the increasing importance being attached to the achievement of food self-sufficiency, particularly for rice and barley. Martin and McDonald (1986) highlight a number of reasons for this development. They include the international price shocks of the early 1970s, which led to rocketing food and oil prices. Combined with a reduction in US food aid, this increased the pressure on Korea's foreign exchange reserves and drew attention to the risks of excessive dependence on international markets. Rapid economic growth in the 1960s had also provided the resources (previously unavailable) to invest in food self-sufficiency.

1976–present

The twin objectives of simultaneously maintaining low prices for consumers and high prices for producers required large public sector subsidies. However, these were fiscally unsustainable and put increasing pressure on macro-economic stability. So, after the mid-1970s, increasing attention was directed at controlling the budgetary costs of agricultural support. The effect of this was that the burden shifted increasingly onto consumers in the form of higher food prices. Policy-makers felt that the now relatively large and wealthy urban population could afford to shoulder these costs.

Over time, support for the agricultural sector has tended to increase. 'In 1980–84, 34 per cent of farm gross domestic product (GDP) resulted from direct and indirect policy-induced transfers' (Diao et al. 2002). Today Korea's agricultural sector is one of the most protected in the world. As a percentage of total farm revenues, the Producer Subsidy Equivalent (PSE), which measures the monetary value of transfers to producers resulting from government subsidies and price support, has become one of the highest in any country. At the end of the 1990s it was double the OECD average (OECD 1999). A large part of these transfers goes towards supporting the production of rice.

High levels of protection have brought Korea into conflict with exporting nations, which have used the WTO to seek greater market access for their own producers. Korean agricultural trade policy, especially in relation to rice, is therefore of considerable interest to negotiators at the WTO's current round of talks.

Impact of agricultural policy

Korea's policy shift at the end of the 1960s clearly had a positive effect on agricultural yields and rural incomes, as well as partial success in achieving self-sufficiency in basic grains.

Effect on production

Table 4 shows a large growth in the output and yields of rice during the 1970s. The average annual output in that decade was 33 per cent higher than in the 1960s. With very little scope for expansion of the area under cultivation, most of this increase came from

---

[1] A measure that compares value added at domestic prices with value added at world prices and hence the effect on producers of government price interventions in input and output markets.

rising yields, which grew by an average of 31 per cent over the decade. However, despite the high levels of support for rice production, growth rates slowed in the following two decades, turning negative in the 1990s.

Table 4: Korean rice production

Average annual production indicators	1961–70	1971–80	1981–90	1991–2000
Area (1,000 ha)	1,189	1,213	1,237	1,095
Output (1,000 mt)	5,011	6,688	7,744	6,981
Yield (mt/ha)	4.2	5.5	6.3	6.4
% growth in relation to previous decade				
Area		2	2	-11
Output		33	16	-10
Yield		31	14	2

Source: FAO 2004

Improvements in agricultural output during the 1970s were also evident for food production as a whole, as can be seen from Figure 2.

Figure 2: Korean food production index

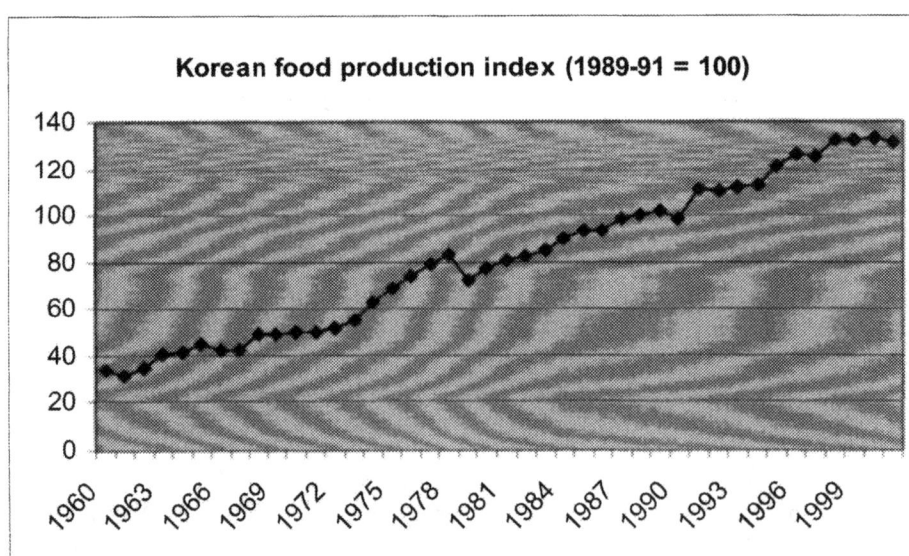

Source: based on data from World Bank Development Indicators 2004

As elsewhere in Asia, improvements in yield were closely linked to the new Green Revolution technologies that were emerging at the time. The government invested heavily in these during the 1970s, providing subsidised inputs and loans, as well as finance for expanded irrigation infrastructure.

Effect on incomes

The endeavour in the 1970s to correct the imbalance between rural and urban incomes also appears to have been relatively successful. 'The annual income of rural households rose above that of urban households in 1974–77 and again in 1982–83. In other years, rural household income was only slightly less than urban levels' (Diao et al. 2002). In terms of reducing rural poverty and rural–urban income inequality, the positive impact of the government's support for agriculture in the 1970s is also confirmed by Adelman and Robinson (1978). However, analysis of the effects of agricultural price support by Moon and Kang (1991) suggests that, within the rural population, the resulting percentage increase in the real income of poorer households may have been small compared with wealthier households. The analysis also suggests that in urban areas the percentage decrease in real incomes arising from the government's price policy was higher for poor urban households than it was for wealthier ones.

Effect on self-sufficiency

The drive towards self-sufficiency has had mixed results. Korea became almost completely self-sufficient in rice by the mid-1980s and in barley by the end of the 1970s, although, as noted earlier, this was done by virtually banning imports and allowing domestic prices to rise (see Figures 3 and 4). Additionally, the government often sought to control domestic demand for these commodities by, for example, banning the use of barley in livestock feed, banning the use of rice for processing, and limiting the use of rice in schools and other public sector institutions (OECD 1999). At the same time, Korea's dependence on imports for other grains increased; it was almost totally dependent on imports for wheat, corn, and soybean. Growing consumer incomes pushed up the demand for meat and, with it, the domestic livestock industry's demand for feed grains. The latter could not be met by domestic production alone.

Figure 3: South Korea – net imports of rice

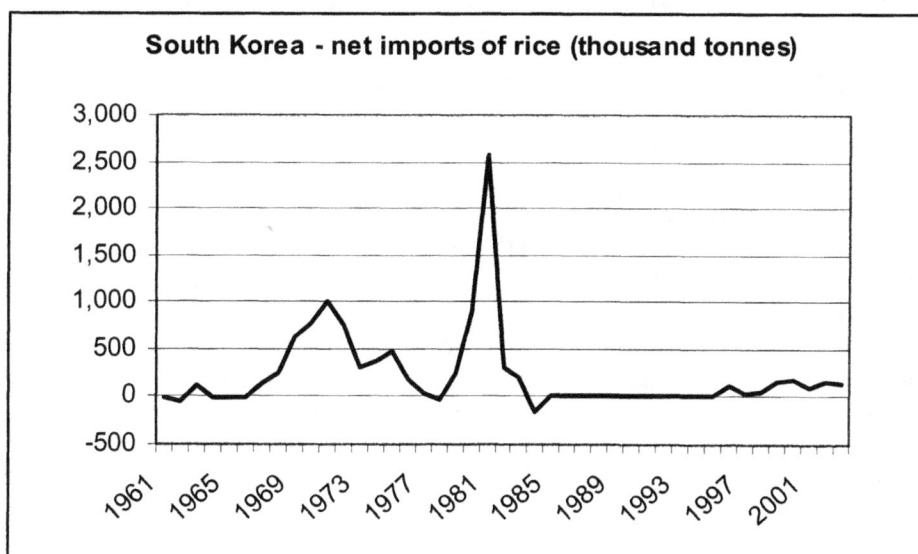

Source: based on data from FAO 2004

Figure 4: South Korea – net imports of barley

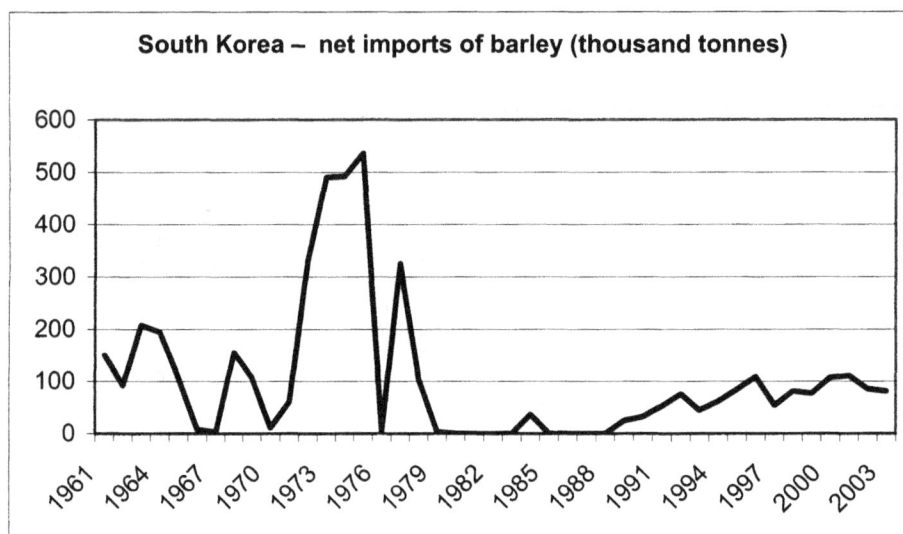

South Korea – net imports of barley (thousand tonnes)

Source: based on data from FAO 2004

Effect on growth

Korea's remarkable economic growth began in the early 1960s. The rural sector's contribution to this was largely as a source of cheap labour for the rapidly growing industrial sector. According to Moon and Kang (1991: 52) '…there is little evidence to suggest that the agricultural sector provided sizeable financial resources for investment in the non-agricultural sectors during the 1950s and 1960s'. Low productivity and neglect of the agricultural sector by policy-makers during this period ensured that there were few surpluses other than those of labour. In addition, the linkages in the 1960s between agriculture as a source of raw materials and industry as a supplier of agricultural inputs were weak. These linkages, had they been stronger, might have fuelled growth in both sectors, but when Korea's economy began to take off, these linkages were largely absent and the industrial sector instead had closer linkages with foreign markets (Byun et al. 1975).

When in the 1970s policy-makers turned their attention to fostering rural development and agricultural sector growth, the industrial sector and the economy as a whole were already growing rapidly. Indeed, over time it was transfers from the non-agricultural sector that increasingly provided the resources needed for growth in the agricultural sector, rather than vice versa (Moon and Kang 1991). This was achieved largely through pricing policies and associated trade protection that kept farm prices above world market levels. According to a number of studies reviewed by Diao et al. (2002), agricultural sector growth has come at the expense of slower overall growth in the economy. The authors' own models suggest that this negative impact has increased over time. Nevertheless, what the agricultural policies introduced in the 1970s do seem to have brought about is a more balanced growth than might otherwise have taken place. Whether these policies have now outlived their usefulness is the question facing Korean policy-makers today.

Malaysia

Economic growth and development

Malaysia's economy has grown rapidly since the 1960s. Annual growth in the 1960s was one of the highest in the region, averaging almost 7 per cent, and 3.5 per cent in per capita terms. The economy grew even faster in the 1970s and has continued to grow rapidly ever since. In 1960, per capita GDP was already considerably higher than in most other countries in the region on account of Malaysia's wealth of natural resources, which included tin as well as agricultural primary commodities, notably rubber. These resources have played a large part in the economy's growth and development, both during the colonial period and subsequently. Malaysia's oil reserves, which allowed the country to become a net exporter in the mid-1970s, have also played an important role. Malaysia has always been an export-oriented economy. In 1960 the value of exports was 55 per cent of total GDP; of this, more than 60 per cent was from rubber and over 17 per cent from tin (Arudsothy 1975). In more recent times Malaysia has diversified away from primary commodities, with manufactured goods now representing about 80 per cent of total exports (World Bank 2005).

The role of agriculture in the economy

Agriculture accounted for about 34 per cent of GDP in the early 1960s, falling to just 9 per cent by 2000. Malaysia is relatively urbanised and so agriculture's contribution to employment has been lower than in most other parts of South-East Asia – 37 per cent in 1980, and falling to 18 per cent in 2000. As noted above, agricultural exports, especially of rubber and, to a lesser extent, palm oil, have historically played an important role in the economy. In the 1960s agricultural raw materials constituted over 50 per cent of total merchandise exports – the largest figure for any country in the survey. However, with the growth of manufacturing and exports of oil, the contribution of agricultural exports had fallen to just over 2 per cent of the total by 2001. Food exports accounted for about 10 per cent of the total in the 1960s, increasing to between 15 and 20 per cent in the 1970s and 1980s, before falling back to below 10 per cent in the 1990s.

As elsewhere in the region, rice is the staple food in Malaysia, although it plays a far smaller role in the agricultural economy owing to the importance of rubber and palm oil. This is reflected in data on the proportions of agricultural land devoted to different crops, as shown in Table 5.

Table 5: Percentage of agricultural area devoted to different crops in 1983

	Rubber	Palm oil	Rice	Coconuts	Cocoa	Other
%	42.4	26.8	14.3	7.4	4.9	4.4

Source: Jenkins and Lai 1991

Nevertheless rice plays a very important role, not only because it is the principal food crop, but also because of its special political significance. Malaysia is an ethnically very mixed society: 54 per cent of the population are Malays, 35 per cent Chinese and 10 per cent Indian (Jenkins and Lai 1991). Economically, the ethnic Chinese are the most powerful group, dominating trade, commerce, and the urban economy. Malays, on the other hand, are more closely associated with the rural economy, farming, and especially rice production. Unlike rubber and palm oil production, rice farming is almost exclusively the preserve of Malay smallholders, and is concentrated in the poorest parts of the country.

Despite their weak position economically, Malays are represented by the most powerful political party, the United Malays National Organization (UMNO), which has dominated government ever since independence. Agricultural policy (and rice policy in particular) has played a large role in the government's objective to increase the Malays' share of the country's wealth – an objective that became particularly important following serious race riots in 1969 (Siamwalla 2001). Reduction of rural poverty was a central feature of the New Economic Policy (NEP) that was adopted in 1971 in response to the ethnic unrest and the inequalities that had sparked it (Wawn 1982). The NEP ushered in a much more interventionist approach to governing both the agricultural sector and the wider economy.

Agricultural policy and trade

The main objectives of government policy on agriculture and agricultural trade have been to generate revenues from agricultural exports, promote self-sufficiency in rice production, stabilise rice prices, and improve the incomes of Malay rice farmers, who represent a disproportionately large proportion of the country's poor.

The rice sector

The government's objectives for the rice sector have been pursued in a number of ways. The main instruments have been control over output prices, input subsidies (especially for fertilisers), and public sector investments in irrigation and land development. The latter were particularly high during the 1960s and early 1970s as the government sought to capitalise on the newly emerging Green Revolution technologies, although they subsequently diminished as the government directed an increasing proportion of its investment budget towards developing the manufacturing and petroleum sectors (Jenkins and Lai 1991).

Malaysia's policy towards staple food prices (i.e. rice prices) has been consistently supportive of producers in seeking to defend a floor price that was comparable with world market prices. In contrast with many other countries, prices were not suppressed in order to provide cheap food for urban consumers. With the introduction of the NEP in the early 1970s, support for producers was increased as both producer and consumer prices were stabilised at above world market levels (Siamwalla 2001; Jenkins and Lai 1991). Instrumental to the escalated support for farmers was the newly formed, state-owned National Paddy and Rice Board (the LPN).

Government price objectives have been pursued by controlling the volume of rice on the domestic market. Since Malaysia is a net importer of rice, domestic prices can be influenced by varying the level of imports. Until 1974 the government achieved this through a system of licences, quotas, and tariffs. Government-managed buffer stocks that were increased or reduced in response to changing market conditions also played a part in controlling rice availability and achieving price objectives.

However in 1974, following the crisis in the world rice market, the government banned private sector imports and handed monopoly control over imports to the LPN, whose trading activities were designed to help achieve the government's price targets. The government also escalated its intervention in the domestic market by greatly expanding the role of the LPN in rice procurement and milling. By 1980 the LPN was handling 33 per cent of domestic rice production (Jenkins and Lai 1991), and between 1973 and 1985 the private sector's share fell from 88 per cent to 54 per cent (Siamwalla 1991). The number of state-owned rice mills increased from just four in 1969 to 31 in 1982. The main losers from the state's expansion into marketing were the private millers and traders, who were mostly Chinese, and who found themselves squeezed out of the market.

Input and credit subsidies have also been a major tool used to support rice smallholders. In 1980 the fertiliser subsidy reached 100 per cent for producers farming 2.4 hectares or less, with the amount of fertiliser required for plots of that size being made available free of charge.

The government rice policy was financed in part by consumers (in the form of higher prices for rice) and also from public sector budgetary transfers. Tax revenues from agricultural exports were more than enough to cover the latter (Jenkins and Lai 1991).

Rubber and palm oil

Rubber and palm oil production has been a major source of revenue for government investment and spending programmes. However, apart from taxing exports, the government has intervened relatively little in either of these sub-sectors, leaving marketing and trade to the private sector.

Plantations account for a large proportion of the production of rubber and palm oil, and foreign as well as Malaysian companies play an important role. In the palm oil sector, foreign companies owned most of the plantations until the 1980s, when the government started buying equity in these companies. The relatively affluent rubber and palm oil sectors have been an obvious source of resources that could be transferred to the rice sector and help to improve the economic status of the country's poorer farmers.

However, in the rubber sector (but not in the palm oil sector) there is also a sizeable number of smallholders involved in production. The incomes of these producers, as well as those of plantation workers, are clearly vulnerable to the effects of export taxes, although labour shortages in the plantation sector caused by rural–urban migration have helped to mitigate the impact on plantation workers. The interests of rubber smallholders have had less influence on government pricing policy than those of rice farmers, partly because they are geographically more dispersed and therefore politically less powerful, and partly because of the importance of rubber export taxes as a source of government revenue. Nevertheless, as the economy has grown and diversified away from agriculture – allowing other sources of government revenue to expand – taxation of the rubber sector has been permitted to fall, thereby reducing some of the pressure on smallholders (Jenkins and Lai 1991).

Performance

Rice

As elsewhere in Asia, the output and yields of rice grew rapidly during the 1970s (see Table 6). The average annual output in the 1970s was 49 per cent higher than in the previous decade. Part of this increase was due to higher yields, but a significant proportion of output growth also came about as a result of expansion of the harvested area, which arose from growth in the cultivated area as well as growth in cropping intensity (the number of harvests derived from a single plot in one year). Government investments in irrigation and land development schemes accounts for much of the growth in the harvested area.

However, the relatively high growth rates of the 1970s were not sustained in the following decade. Yields stagnated, and most of the land that was suitable for irrigation had already been developed, providing little scope for further increases in the cultivated area (Jenkins and Lai 1991). The 1990s saw some improvement, although the pace of change was not as great as during the 1970s, when agriculture and rural development were considered major priorities and output was benefiting from the adoption of new, high-yielding seed varieties.

Table 6: Malaysian rice production

Average annual production indicators	1961–70	1971–80	1981–90	1991–2000
Area (1,000 ha)	597	724	666	686
Output (1,000 mt)	1,291	1,926	1,762	2,078
Yield (mt/ha)	2.2	2.7	2.6	3.0
% growth in relation to previous decade				
Area		21	-8	3
Output		49	-8	18
Yield		23	-1	14

Source: FAOSTAT 2004

The output improvements during the 1970s did reduce Malaysia's dependence on rice imports. The country imported less in the 1970s than it did in the 1960s, although it never achieved complete self-sufficiency, and overall level of imports rose again in the 1980s and 1990s (see Figure 5).

Figure 5: Malaysia – net imports of rice

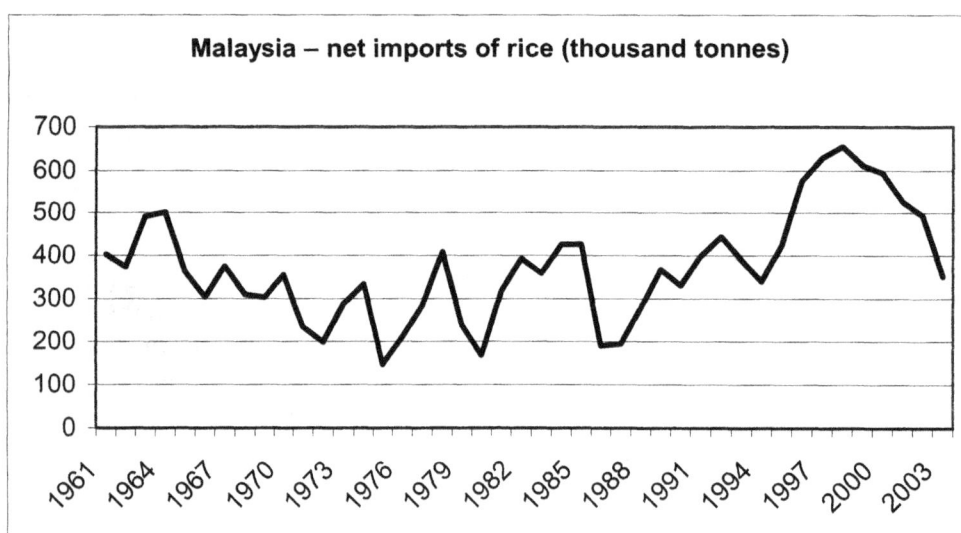

Source: based on data from FAO 2004

Rubber and palm oil performance

Malaysia has used export taxes to stabilise prices and generate public sector revenues. By varying the level of taxation, policy-makers have to some extent been able to insulate producers from the very large price fluctuations that are a feature of international commodity markets. Over the longer term, the size of the tax has also reflected the desire to achieve an appropriate balance between the generation of revenues, and not overly undermine the production on which these revenues depend. Malaysia appears to have been reasonably successful in achieving such a balance, even though taxes have at times been quite high (Jenkins and Lai 1991). Moreover, whilst a large amount of the government revenue from export crops has been directed towards supporting the rice sector, a significant amount of it has been reinvested in the export sector itself, helping to fund agricultural research and tree- replanting programmes, and ensuring that the sector remains internationally competitive.

During the 1970s, when resources were being transferred to the rice sector, the rubber and oil palm sub-sectors were expanding too, helped by a boom in international commodity prices. There were large yield improvements in the rubber sector and significant yield improvements too in the oil palm sector. The area devoted to oil palm increased massively as new land was opened up for its cultivation. Output and yield improvements in the oil palm sector continued to improve in the 1980s and 1990s, albeit at a slower rate. However, rubber production began to stagnate in the 1980s and actually declined in the 1990s, as land was gradually transferred to oil palm production. With the declining relative profitability of rubber, oil palm has now superseded it in terms of the area devoted to each (see Tables 7 and 8).

Table 7: Malaysian rubber production

Average annual production indicators	1961–70	1971–80	1981–90	1991–2000
Area (1,000 ha)	1,410	1,730	1,592	1,471
Output (1,000 mt)	980	1,503	1,505	1,033
Yield (mt/ha)	0.7	0.9	0.9	0.7
% growth in relation to previous decade				
Area		23	-8	-8
Output		53	0	-31
Yield		25	9	-26

Source: FAO 2004

Table 8: Malaysian oil palm production

Average annual production indicators	1961–70	1971–80	1981–90	1991–2000
Area (1,000 ha)	77	444	1,270	2,336
Output (1,000 mt)	1,058	6,878	22,140	43,254
Yield (mt/ha)	13.7	15.5	17.4	18.5
% growth in relation to previous decade				
Area		476	186	84
Output		550	222	95
Yield		13	12	6

Source: FAO 2004

Poverty and growth

Agricultural exports, especially rubber, have clearly been a major driving force in the growth of the Malaysian economy. Within the agricultural sector, they have helped to finance investments in productivity-enhancing technologies in the staple food sector, and have contributed to raising the incomes of poor farmers in the rice sector. They have also provided surpluses for public and private sector investments outside the agricultural sector, and have undoubtedly made a major contribution to the rapid growth of manufacturing since the 1980s.

The government's role in facilitating the transfer of resources from the more prosperous sectors of the economy to poorer groups, most notably Malay smallholders, also helped to reduce the risk of ethnic conflict and social unrest, which could so easily have undermined the country's progress during a critical phase of its development.

Viet Nam

Economic growth and development

Viet Nam stands out amongst the countries surveyed in this study for a number of important reasons. Firstly, unlike the others, it was until recently a centrally planned economy with collectivised agricultural production. It is also the most recent country to 'take off' and enter a period of rapid and sustained economic growth; it therefore remains the most rural and agricultural economy in the sample. Finally, it is the only country in the survey to have become a major exporter of its main staple food commodity, namely rice.

The economy began to take off after 1986 when the government announced a major policy shift (known as Doi Moi). This set in motion the transition from a centrally planned command economy to a market-oriented system involving a much greater role for the private sector, greater openness to international trade and foreign investment, and a more export-oriented approach to industrial growth. Doi Moi also renewed the emphasis on growth in the agricultural sector.

In 1986, GDP per capita in Viet Nam was just $189. However, between 1986 and 2003, it grew by over 5 per cent per annum and by 2003 had reached $438.[2] During the 1990s the economy as a whole grew by almost 8 per cent a year.

The role of agriculture in the economy

In 1991 agriculture accounted for about 40 per cent of GDP and 75 per cent of employment. As the economy has grown, these figures have fallen: by 2002 agricultural value added was only 23 per cent of GDP and at the end of the 1990s the sector's contribution to employment was just under 70 per cent. Nevertheless, agriculture continues to play a much greater role in the national economy than is the case in any of the other countries examined in this survey.

Rice is by far the single most important commodity in Viet Nam. Other agricultural products, such as coffee, maize, and livestock, are also of significance, especially in non-rice growing regions; however, this study will focus on rice. It accounts for 75 per cent of calorific intake and 30 per cent of total consumption expenditure. It is produced by about 75 per cent of the country's labour force, covers 78 per cent of annual crop land, and in 1999 accounted for over half the value of all exports (Ryan 1999). In 2000 rice represented 43 per cent of the total value of agricultural output, and Viet Nam is now the world's fifth largest rice producer. In 1989, after many decades of being a net importer of rice, Viet Nam became a net exporter and quickly advanced to the position of being the world's second largest rice exporter after Thailand (Nguyen and Grote 2004). Rice policy is of fundamental importance to the rural economy, to the economy at large, and to the fight against poverty.

Two-thirds of rice production is concentrated in two relatively small, but densely populated, regions: the Mekong River Delta in the south, which accounts for more than half of the country's rice production, and the Red River Delta in the north, which is one of the most densely populated agricultural areas in the world (Minot and Goletti 2000). Other regions of the country (much of which is mountainous, sparsely populated, and

---

[2] Based on the 1995 US$ value.

unsuited to rice cultivation) depend upon surpluses from these two regions for their food security.

The evolution of agricultural policy

Viet Nam's agriculture policy in recent times is marked by two outstanding features – the de-collectivisation of agricultural production and the government's changing position on rice exports. Reforms in both these areas have been responsible for rapid growth in agricultural production over the past two decades (Minot and Goletti 2000; Benjamin and Brandt 2001).

The evolution of agricultural policy in Viet Nam since unification at the end of the war in 1975 began with government attempts to collectivise agriculture in the south (a process undertaken in the north two decades earlier). However, opposition to this process by southern farmers contributed to the sector's poor performance over the next five years, causing the government to revise its policy on collectivisation and to introduce the 'contract system'. Under this system, which came into being in 1981, farmers were allocated plots of land and contracted by the collectives to supply a specified volume of output at the official government price. Farmers were allowed to sell any surplus above the contracted amount on the open market, although at this time consumer prices were still largely determined by government policy, which was to keep prices low, through subsidies where necessary.

Farmers responded well to the contract system and output rose until the mid-1980s, when hyperinflation set in, eroding the real value of the official procurement price that farmers were receiving for an increasingly large proportion of their production. Incentives were undermined and production stagnated (Minot and Goletti 2000). The announcement in 1986 of the new market-oriented Doi Moi policy was intended to address these and other economic problems.

By 1989 the farm household was officially recognised as the basic agricultural production unit, compulsory purchases by the state had been eliminated, and private traders were permitted to buy direct from farmers (Minot and Goletti 2000). Reforms in the late 1980s and early 1990s further strengthened producers' rights over their plots and their output. Over the same period, domestic and foreign trade in agricultural commodities and inputs (notably fertiliser) was increasingly liberalised and, although state-owned enterprises (SOEs) continued to play a major part in the agricultural economy, direct intervention by the government in agricultural marketing and price setting declined. Many of the subsidies provided to SOEs (and, through them, to farmers or consumers) were reduced or removed as the government tightened fiscal policy in an effort to control inflation (Ryan 1999).

Nevertheless, the level of prices and price stability remained important policy concerns for rice, fertiliser, and a few other key commodities. In the case of rice, the government continued to defend a floor price for producers and a ceiling price for consumers, through strategic government procurement activities, and through continued control over rice exports and domestic long-distance rice trade. Through most of the 1990s, SOEs continued to monopolise exports and domestic long-distance trade. The latter, which relates primarily to trade between the south and north of the country, was as heavily regulated as external trade (Minot and Goletti 2000).

In 1993 rice was the only commodity that was still subject to government export quotas. Policy-makers feared that higher and more volatile prices resulting from complete liberalisation would harm consumers, especially those living in the poorer parts of the country that depended upon cheap surpluses from the delta regions. The government's reluctance to remove export restrictions has been linked to Viet Nam's experience with exports under the French and Japanese administrations during the first part of the twentieth century. At that time large-scale exports coincided with famine and food shortages and were strongly associated with reductions in domestic consumption (Minot and Goletti, 2000).

Despite its reservations, the government did gradually increase the rice export quota during the 1990s. In 1992 the official export quota was less than 1m tonnes. This rose to 4.5m tonnes in 1998 but fell back to 3.9m tonnes in 1999, before rising again to 4.3m tonnes in 2000. Then in 2001 the quota system was abolished altogether. Additionally, towards the end of the 1990s, the statutory monopoly of SOEs over rice exports was officially ended and the legal barriers to private sector involvement in the domestic long-distance trade in rice were also lifted. Nevertheless, SOEs have continued to dominate both of these trades subsequently.

Impact of agricultural policy

It seems evident that the policy reforms introduced since the early 1980s have had a major impact on the performance of the agricultural sector, although the introduction of the contract system at the beginning of the 1980s also played an important part.

Rice production and trade

According to Benjamin and Brandt (2001), one the most important effects of market liberalisation and the lowering of export barriers was to increase rice prices – in all regions, but especially in the south, where the effects of policy changes were to depress prices in relation to those received by producers in the north. Examining changes between 1993 and 1998, these two authors also highlight the change in fertiliser prices which 'fell dramatically in all regions'. They attribute this to the liberalisation of fertiliser imports, which led to a three-fold increase in the volume of imports and a sharp increase in domestic availability. Viet Nam is heavily dependent upon fertiliser imports.

These changes in the price of inputs and outputs increased production incentives and helped to stimulate rapid growth in agricultural output, particularly in the case of rice, as can be seen from Table 9.

Table 9: Viet Nam rice production

Average annual production indicators	1961–70	1971–80	1981–90	1991–2000
Area (1,000 ha)	4,797	5,190	5,737	6,949
Output (1,000 mt)	9,244	10,886	15,926	25,953
Yield (mt/ha)	1.9	2.1	2.8	3.7
% growth in relation to previous decade				
Area		8	11	21
Output		18	46	63
Yield		9	32	35

Source: FAO 2004

The output of rice grew relatively slowly during the 1970s – not surprisingly perhaps, given the disruption caused by war and the subsequent problems of reconstruction and reunification. However, output and yields grew rapidly in the 1980s and even faster in the 1990s. The increased production of rice, combined with the reduction in government export restrictions, is reflected in a sharp rise in the volume of exports from the end of the 1980s onwards, as can be seen from Figure 6.

Figure 6: Viet Nam – net exports of rice

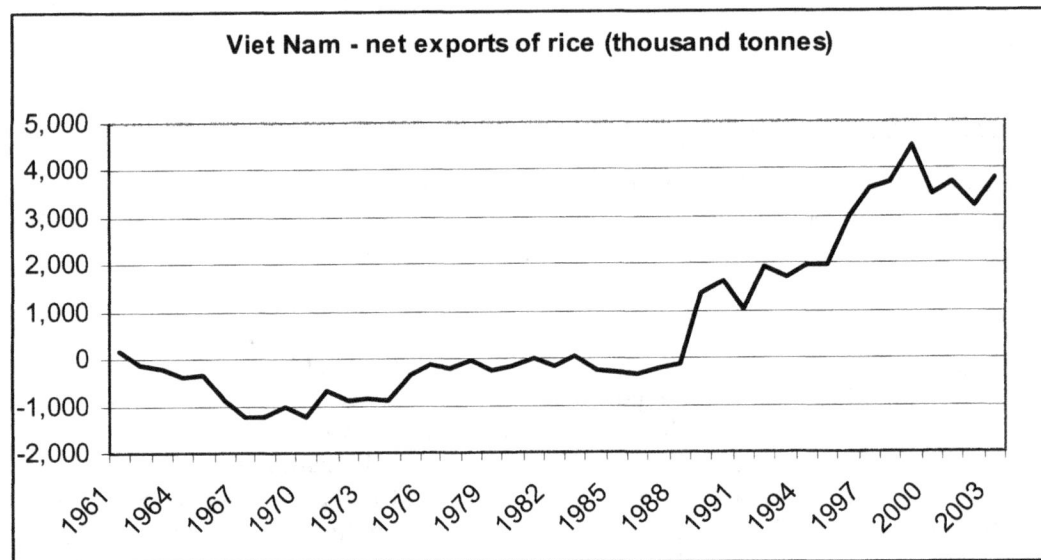

Source: based on data from FAO 2004

Economic growth and poverty reduction

During the 1990s agricultural value added grew at a rate of almost 5 per cent per year. Since at the beginning of the decade agriculture accounted for about 40 per cent of GDP, its direct contribution to overall growth in the economy is obviously significant, even though its proportional contribution has fallen as the economy has diversified away from agriculture. Increasing productivity in the agricultural sector has also contributed to economic growth by allowing resources (land, labour, and capital) to be released for use in other sectors of the economy, which have been rapidly expanding since the beginning of the 1990s.

The potential effects of agricultural sector liberalisation on poverty have been among the major concerns of policy-makers in Viet Nam, especially in relation to the impact of higher rice prices. In the short term the people most vulnerable to higher rice prices are those who spend a large proportion of their income on rice, namely the urban poor and the rural poor (especially ethnic minorities in the highland regions) who do not grow enough rice to meet their own needs. Conversely, the main beneficiaries of higher rice prices have been those producers who produce a marketable surplus. Since the latter category represents a large proportion of the country's poor, the overall effect on poverty of market liberalisation in the rice sector has been positive (Benjamin and Brandt 2001; Minot and Goletti 2000). At a national level, the proportion of the population falling below the national poverty line[3] fell from 58 per cent in 1993 to 37 per cent in 1998 and 28 per cent in 2002.[4]

Two important factors have been emphasised as being important in maximising the contribution of rice sector liberalisation (and associated price increases) to economic growth and poverty reduction. One relates to equality in land distribution and the other to government investment in infrastructure and technology (Minot and Goletti 2000; Ahmed and Goletti 1997).

In Viet Nam only 2 per cent of the rural population are landless, compared with 20 per cent in other Asian countries (Minot and Goletti 2000: 91). The benefits of rice price rises are therefore distributed more evenly – not only in the form of higher incomes for smallholders (who represent the majority of the poor), but also because the surpluses resulting from growth in their incomes are more likely to be spent/invested in rural areas (where most poor people live). This has the effect of increasing incomes in the non-farming sector, including those of consumers who may initially lose out from having to pay higher prices for rice.

The ability of farmers to respond to higher prices depends critically on their access to the technology and know-how required to raise yields. Relatively high levels of education and literacy amongst Vietnamese farmers (compared with other poor countries), combined with heavy government investment in irrigation and agricultural extension services prior to market liberalisation, have allowed farmers successfully to adopt modern technologies, such as high-yielding seed varieties, fertilisers and crop protection methods.

Although the level of subsidy is hard to measure, government efforts to promote self-sufficiency in rice throughout the first half of the 1980s appear to have provided a strong platform for growth, even though in subsequent years growth seems to have been largely driven by market liberalisation. Some (but not all) estimates suggest that, from the mid-1990s onwards, the net effect of government intervention in the rice sector, as well as in the agricultural sector as a whole, has shifted from negative to positive protection and support, although the overall effect is still considered small (Nguyen and Grote 2004).

---

[3] Based on the income required to meet basic needs, including the consumption of 2,100 calories per day.

[4] Vietnam Development Report 2004.

Chile

Economic growth and development

In Chile, as elsewhere in Latin America, the process of economic expansion and development began earlier than in developing countries in other parts of the world. By 1960, per capita GDP already stood at $1,968,[5] and almost 70 per cent of the population lived in urban areas. Today 87 per cent of the population live in towns or cities (World Bank 2005). Chile is rich in mineral resources and is the world's largest producer of copper – a commodity that has played an important role in the growth of the country's economy. In 1973 copper represented 82 per cent of the total value of exports (Hachette and Rozas 1993), although, with the decline in world copper prices and the increase in agricultural exports, this figure has since fallen.

Chile's economy has been one of Latin America's more successful ones in recent decades. Growth was slower than the regional average in the 1960s and 1970s, but began to take off in the late 1970s, following the start of major economic restructuring in 1974. Before that, Chile's development policy (as in many other developing countries at the time) was inward-looking, focusing on the expansion of domestic industry behind protective trade barriers and involving deep and widespread government intervention in the economy. A major economic crisis developed between 1970 and 1973, as attempts by the government of President Allende to nationalise large parts of the economy disrupted production and led to spiralling inflation. Towards the end of 1973 a military coup headed by General Pinochet paved the way for structural adjustment and a market-oriented economy, in which the liberalisation of international trade, the deregulation of domestic markets, and privatisation became central features.

The economy responded positively to these economic reforms, although progress was temporarily halted in 1982–83 when the country was hit by the severest recession in its history, owing to a major slowdown in the global economy. Nevertheless, per capita GDP grew at an average annual rate of 2.1 per cent in the 1980s and 4.9 per cent in the 1990s, compared with only 1.8 per cent in the 1960s and 1.2 per cent in the 1970s.

The role of agriculture in the economy

Compared with other countries in the study, agriculture plays a relatively small role in Chile's economy. Its contribution was 9 per cent in 1960 and has now returned to about this level, after having dipped slightly below it in the late 1960s and early 1970s. Amongst those countries surveyed, only Botswana's agricultural sector makes a smaller proportional contribution to GDP. The sector's contribution to employment was 30 per cent in 1960 (Hachette and Rozas 1993), falling to 14 per cent by 2002. However, agriculture's relatively small contribution to GDP and employment belies its importance to the rest of the economy as a determinant of real wages and, more recently, as a source of export revenues. Real wages are affected by the price of food, which in the 1960s and 1970s accounted for 50 per cent of the total expenditure of people in the lowest income quintile and 40 per cent of the expenditure by all but the rich (Valdés et al. 1991).

In contrast with other countries in the sample, agriculture's contribution to exports has increased, largely as a result of the reforms that began in the mid-1970s. The proportion of total merchandise exports accounted for by agricultural raw materials increased from

---

[5] Expressed in 1995 US$.

about 2 per cent in the 1960s to over 10 per cent in 2000, while the proportion accounted for by food exports increased from about 6 per cent to more than 25 per cent over the same period.

Chile's agricultural sector can be divided into a traditional sector that competes with imports and a modern export-oriented sector. The latter consists mainly of horticultural products, whilst the former is based around wheat (the single most important crop), maize, livestock, and other food staples. The export sector expanded rapidly after 1974 although, because of the intensive nature of production in this sector, the area allocated to it is a relatively small proportion of the total (see Figure 7).

Figure 7: Allocation of agricultural land by product

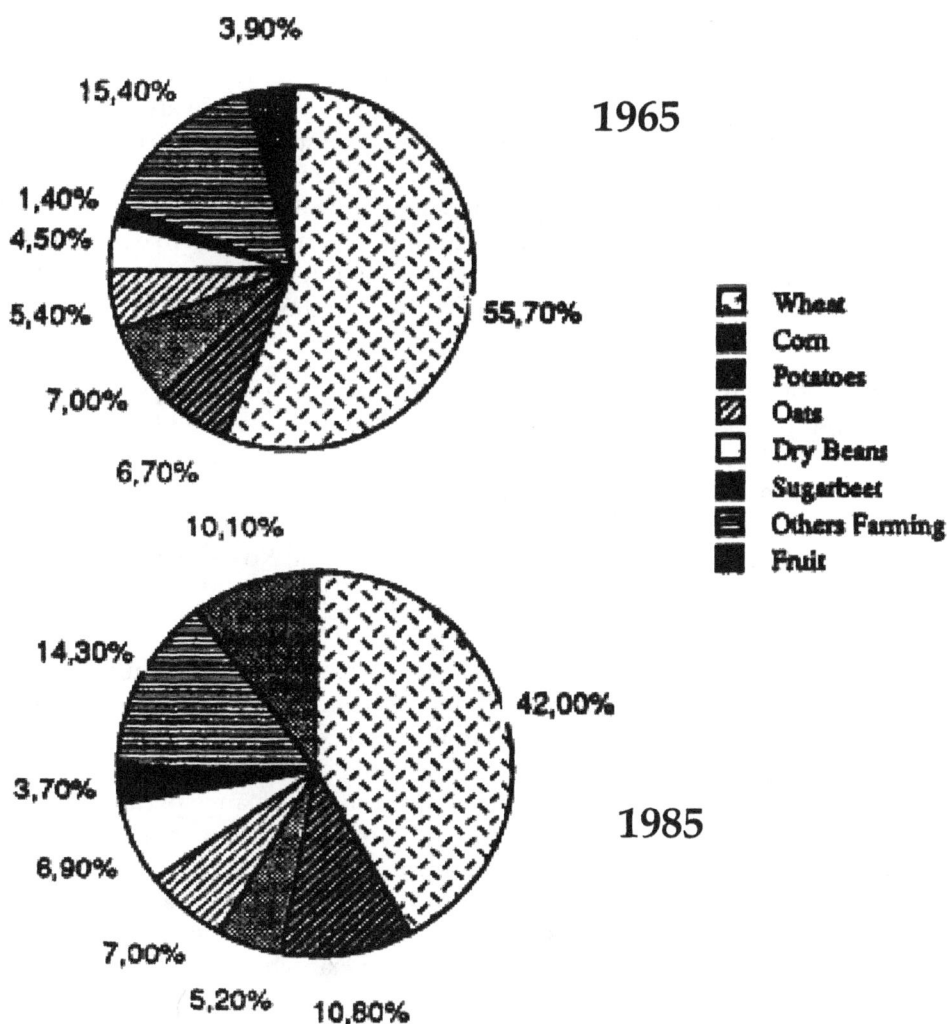

Source: Hachette and Rozas 1993

Agricultural exports consist mainly of fresh fruits, wine, and processed horticultural products. Some of Chile's recent success as an agricultural exporter can be attributed to its unique geography:

- The country is over 4,000km long from north to south, but is on average less than 200km wide. This gives rise to a wide range of agro-climatic zones, allowing the country to produce both temperate and Mediterranean crops.

- The natural borders of the Pacific Ocean in the west and the Andes mountains in the east make it easier to control trans-boundary pests and diseases that undermine production and which are an obstacle to exports into the rich northern countries where health and sanitary regulations are strict.

- Being in the southern hemisphere allows Chile to exploit markets in the northern hemisphere during seasons when there is little competition from northern hemisphere producers.

Agricultural policy and trade – evolution and reform

Pre-reform policy

Prior to 1974 the main thrust of agricultural policy was to provide cheap food to the growing urban sector, thereby reducing pressure on wages in the industrial sector, and helping to promote industrial growth. Food self-sufficiency was also an important policy goal. There were times when the government sought to improve the agricultural terms of trade with the rest of the economy by raising the price paid to producers and subsidising farm credit and inputs, especially from the mid-1960s onwards. However, the net effect of policy overall was a disincentive to agricultural production, since an overvalued exchange rate and the much higher levels of protection offered to the industrial sector reduced agricultural prices relative to those elsewhere in the economy (Valdés et al. 1991).

Direct intervention in the nominal price of agricultural commodities was exerted through trade restrictions combined with interventions in the domestic market by state marketing boards, such as the ECA. In addition to its powers to intervene in domestic markets, the ECA also had a monopoly over imports of wheat, fertiliser, and many other agricultural commodities. International trade by the private sector was controlled through a variety of tariffs, quotas, and other non-tariff barriers (Hachette and Rozas 1993).

Structural adjustment

After 1974, agricultural policy was shaped by the reforms taking place throughout the economy. On the one hand, these reforms reflected the immediate need to reduce inflation, cut the budget deficit, and deal with the balance of payments problem: this required a sharp tightening of fiscal and monetary policy combined with exchange rate devaluation. However, the reforms also reflected a complete change of direction in relation to the country's long-term development strategy – one in which market forces rather than the state were to play the leading role in determining the way resources should be allocated. In agriculture, as elsewhere, domestic and international trade were liberalised and public sector subsidies and services, including access to cheap credit and farm inputs, were cut. Most farm service parastatals, meanwhile, were privatised.

Whilst most prices in the economy were liberalised almost immediately, domestic price controls for basic agricultural commodities and foodstuffs were liberalised more slowly. For a few years the ECA continued to intervene in the domestic market to achieve price targets, with the aid of government subsidies. However, its operations were gradually wound down as the private sector expanded its role and market forces began to determine prices. The government's strategy for influencing domestic agricultural prices shifted to trade policy instruments, especially tariffs and import duties.

Trade policy reforms

The government that came to power in 1973 eliminated most non-tariff barriers to agricultural and non-agricultural trade and simplified the existing tariff system by replacing the numerous different tariff rates with a unified rate covering most goods. By 1979 this had been reduced to 10 per cent, although it was to rise again in the early 1980s, reaching 35 per cent, before falling back to 15 per cent towards the end of the 1980s (Hachette and Rozas 1993). In 2003 the average tariff rate was 6 per cent (Muchnik and Camhi 2003).

The 'uniform tariff equivalent' is an indicator used to measure the effects on trade of protectionist policies. It is the tariff that would maintain the same volume of trade as existing protectionist policies and is estimated by Valdés et al. (1991) to have fallen from a range of 39–95 per cent during the 1960s and the first half of the 1970s to 10–33 per cent in the following decade. Most agricultural protection after 1974 was targeted at a few key importables: wheat, sugar, oilseeds, and dairy products, which benefited from additional import duties and surcharges over and above the basic *ad valorem* tariff referred to above. For example, additional duties applied to imports of milk and milk derivatives have at times raised the nominal protection rate for these products to about 50 per cent (Hachette and Rozas 1993).

Another important feature of domestic pricing policy for much of the post-1974 period has been the price band system for wheat, sugar, and oilseeds. It involves a band within which prices are permitted to fluctuate, and serves to stabilise domestic prices and protect the country's producers from international price volatility. It operates through the defence of a floor price and a maximum ceiling price for each commodity and requires both that additional import tariffs be applied when the floor is reached and that a tariff rebate be applied to prevent the ceiling from being exceeded. The system has recently been challenged by Argentina on the grounds that it conflicts with Chile's WTO commitments, and it is also threatened by negotiations for a free trade agreement with the USA.

The development of exports became a central part of agricultural policy after 1974. The main approach to achieving this lay in the removal of existing obstacles, such as an overvalued exchange rate, taxes, export quotas, prohibitions, and other bureaucratic obstacles. Market forces were allowed to determine the pattern and level of exports. There were no explicit export subsidies and, although the sector has benefited from tax rebates and government-funded export promotion activities, these are not considered to represent a particularly large subsidy (Hachette and Rozas 1993). Investor confidence in the government's commitment to an export-oriented strategy and to the protection of property rights has been highlighted as one of the most important reasons for export success, equalling or exceeding the positive effect of price incentives, which also increased significantly (Valdés et al. 1991; Hachette and Rozas 1993).

Land reform

The ownership of land in Chile has always been highly concentrated. In the 1960s about 55 per cent of all arable land was in the hands of large landowners and three-quarters of all agricultural land was owned by about 7 per cent of farms (Hachette and Rozas 1993). A number of land reform initiatives were undertaken in the 1960s and early 1970s. However, the redistribution of land, which accelerated after 1970, was poorly managed and became increasingly chaotic, as the government intensified efforts to hand over control of large farms to workers' co-operatives. Large areas of land were also seized illegally. The resulting uncertainties regarding property rights contributed greatly to the decline in agricultural production during the early 1970s (Valdés et al. 1991; Hachette and Rozas 1993). The new government that took power at the end of this period was committed to reinstating the supremacy of private property rights, and many of the agrarian reforms and land expropriations that had taken place over the previous decade were reversed. This helped to boost production, but undid some of the improvements in equality of land tenure. Some estimates suggest that more than half of the small farmers who gained land under agrarian reforms subsequently lost it again after 1973 (Berdegué 2002).

Impact of reforms

Agricultural performance

In the post-1974 era agricultural prices improved significantly, relative to prices in other sectors of the economy. This came about largely as a result of exchange rate devaluation and lower levels of industrial protection (Valdés et al. 1991), and clearly had a positive impact on the performance of the agricultural sector, which was markedly better after 1973 than before.

The value of agricultural output dropped sharply during the early 1970s and was lower in 1973 than it was in 1960. However, even in the decade up to 1970, the annual growth in agricultural output averaged less than 2 per cent. Between 1974 and 2003, by contrast, output grew at an average annual rate of 3.7 per cent, although the rate of growth slowed during the 1990s – between 1974 and 1990 the rate of growth was 4.7 per cent.

Agricultural policy reforms have also turned Chile into a large net exporter of agricultural commodities. The country's agricultural trade balance turned positive in 1985 and the surplus has grown steadily ever since (see Figure 8). The value of non-traditional agricultural exports has grown by between 300 and 600 per cent since the mid-1980s, while over the same period the area devoted to traditional food staples destined for the domestic market has declined by one-third because of a decline in their real price (Berdegué 2002).

Figure 8: Chile – agricultural trade surplus

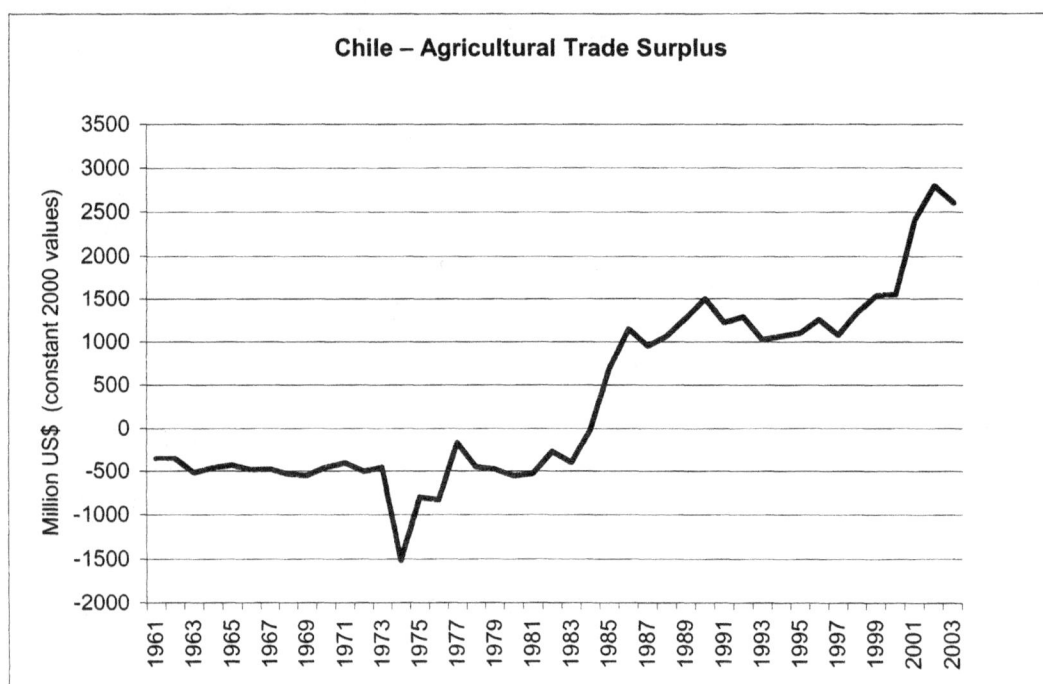

Source: FAO 2004

Agricultural Trade Policy in Developing Countries During Take-Off
Oxfam GB Research Report, July 2006

Despite the decline in area devoted to staple food crops, the output of these has increased significantly owing to the rapid improvement in yields experienced in the 1980s and 1990s. The figures for wheat and maize in Tables 10 and 11 demonstrate this clearly.

Table 10: Chile wheat production

Average annual production indicators	1961–70	1971–80	1981–90	1991–2000
Area (1,000 ha)	745	624	509	397
Output (1,000 mt)	1,170	1,019	1,279	1,440
Yield (mt/ha)	1.6	1.6	2.5	3.6
% growth in relation to previous decade				
Area		-16	-18	-22
Output		-13	26	13
Yield		4	54	44

Source: FAOSTAT 2004

Table 11: Chile maize production

Average annual production indicators	1961–70	1971–80	1981–90	1991–2000
Area (1,000 ha)	82	100	113	97
Output (1,000 mt)	238	329	671	856
Yield (mt/ha)	2.9	3.3	5.9	8.8
% growth in relation to previous decade				
Area		22	14	-15
Output		38	104	28
Yield		13	80	49

Source: FAO 2004

Smallholders and poverty

While the agricultural sector as a whole, and the export sector in particular, have clearly benefited from liberalisation, it is not entirely clear to what extent smallholders have shared in these benefits directly. Most production in the export sector, and a sizeable proportion of production in the traditional sector, takes place on large commercial farms, using modern technologies applied to relatively fertile soils. Smallholders, on the other hand, rely mainly on livestock and traditional food crops, have very small plots, make little use of modern inputs, and are concentrated in areas where the land is less fertile. Relatively few of them produce a marketable surplus, and indeed a large proportion do not even produce enough to meet household subsistence needs and are therefore dependent on off-farm employment.

It is suggested that the price stability achieved by the price band system may have contributed to productivity increases and greater social and economic stability in those sectors and regions where the rural poor are concentrated, although its positive effects cannot easily be separated from other factors relating to improvements in the wider economy (Hachette and Rozas 1993). It is likely that the rural poor as a whole have benefited more from the increase in rural employment opportunities – both on-farm and off-farm – resulting from agricultural sector growth, than they have as smallholders. Since the agricultural export sector is much more labour-intensive than the traditional sector, the growth in rural employment opportunities has undoubtedly been greatest in those regions where production for export is concentrated.

Those who have not benefited directly from economic reform have been targeted by social safety net programmes, which have been an important feature of government efforts to tackle poverty in both rural and urban areas. The main programmes have related to health, nutrition, and education, including feeding programmes aimed at reducing childhood malnutrition.

There have also been a number of programmes aimed at small farmers, offering cheap loans and technical assistance (Muchnik and Camhi 2003). Support for smallholder farming – and, in particular, efforts to encourage smallholder diversification away from traditional commodities – has been given renewed emphasis by the government since the early 1990s. The strategy has revolved around the formation of farmer organisations (known as EACs), which provide their members with marketing, processing, and other value-adding services and which act as an interface between farmers and public and private sector service providers. Approximately a fifth of all Chilean small farmers were members of such organisations by 1998, although the main concentration of such organisations was in the milk sub-sector. The strategy has had mixed results, it seems, with only about 20 per cent of EACs performing well, compared with 50 per cent that continue to depend upon external financial support and 30 per cent that have failed completely (Berdegué 2002).

Nationally, poverty levels appear to have declined significantly in recent decades. In 1987 the proportion of the population living on less than one dollar a day was 6 per cent, falling to 2 per cent by 2000 (World Bank 2005). The proportion of the population living below the two dollar a day poverty line fell from 24 per cent to 10 per cent over the same period. Figures for the pre-reform period are not available, but the statistics paint a fairly positive picture in relation to the poverty impact of the post-1974 policy environment.

Economic growth

Chile has enjoyed relatively high rates of economic growth since it embarked on its structural adjustment reforms in the mid-1970s. Policy reforms in the agricultural sector and in the wider economy have contributed to this growth. In contrast with other rapidly growing economies, the contribution of agriculture to Chile's economy has remained stable, rather than declining over time. This is consistent with the shift from the industrial bias of development policies prior to the mid-1970s to a more market-oriented approach that has allowed Chile to take greater advantage of its agricultural potential. Agriculture's direct contribution to the economy is small relative to other sectors. Nevertheless, by acting as a stimulus to rural service providers, rural labour markets, and other industrial sectors, agricultural growth has undoubtedly been responsible for some of the growth that has taken place elsewhere in the economy.

Botswana

Economic growth and development

Botswana stands out as one of the only countries in sub-Saharan African to have experienced rapid economic growth since the 1960s. In 1960 its GDP per capita was well below the average for the region, and by 2003 it was almost ten times the average. The main stimulus for Botswana's rapid growth was the discovery of diamonds in 1967, which immediately lifted the annual per capita growth rate from just under 3.5 per cent during 1960–67 to just under 14 per cent during 1967–74. The economy continued to grow rapidly over the following two decades. Per capita GDP grew by just over 11 per cent per annum in the 1970s, and by just over 7 per cent in the 1980s, before dropping back to just under 2 per cent in the 1990s.

Botswana's economy is very open, with exports and imports in 1994 each being equal to about 60 per cent of GDP (Lado 2001). Botswana is now the world's largest exporter of diamonds in value terms.

The role of agriculture in the economy

In the early 1960s the contribution of agriculture to Botswana's economy was very high. At 41 per cent of GDP in 1960, and averaging over 35 per cent over the next decade, it was considerably higher than the sub-Saharan Africa average of about 25 per cent during the 1960s. However, since the discovery of diamonds, the relative contribution of agriculture has fallen dramatically. By 2002 it represented just 2 per cent of GDP – less than for any of the other countries reviewed in this study. Agriculture's contribution to exports – which, again, are dominated by diamonds – is also extremely low: less than 1 per cent in the case of agricultural raw materials and about 3 per cent in the case of food exports.

Before the development of the diamond sector, and more recently tourism, the country's main export was beef, which remains the single most important agricultural export. In 1998 beef accounted for about 7 per cent of Botswana's total export revenues, compared with over 70 per cent provided by diamonds (Lado 2001).

Botswana is an arid, sparsely populated country and much of its surface area is far better suited to livestock husbandry than it is to arable farming. Although the country is a net exporter of beef, it has always been a net importer of staple food commodities, such as sorghum and maize, which together account for over 90 per cent of domestic cereal production. In a normal year Botswana produces only about 30 per cent of its annual cereal requirements (Lado 2001). In production terms, sorghum is traditionally the most important crop and the one best suited to Botswana's agro-climatic conditions. In the 1960s relatively little maize was grown, although its share in cereal production has grown in recent decades in response to increasing demand, despite it being a more risky crop. Maize now accounts for a larger proportion of domestic cereal consumption than does sorghum, with the shortfall relative to demand being made up through imports.

Although agriculture's contribution to both GDP and exports is now very small, the sector remains the main source of income for about half of the population, demonstrating that the proceeds of rapid economic growth have not been equally distributed (Thirtle et al. 2003). There is a large gap between rural and urban incomes, and in rural areas, where up to 70 per cent of the population still live, poverty remains widespread (Lado 2001; OECD/AfDB 2002).

Agricultural policy and trade

Botswana's policy on agriculture and agricultural trade is best understood by looking at policy in the staple food sector and policy in the beef sector. The country has always had a very open trade policy in relation to both of these sectors, and even prior to the discovery of diamonds the state did not endeavour to control the agricultural economy to the degree that many other African countries have done (Hope 1998).

Food security versus food self-sufficiency

Before 1991, food self-sufficiency, particularly in relation to sorghum and maize, was a key objective of agricultural policy, despite the fact that only a relatively small proportion of the country is suitable for crop production. However, in contrast with many other countries in sub-Saharan Africa, strategies to encourage domestic agricultural production have generally operated within a liberal trading regime and have not included major restrictions on agricultural imports. Even prior to 1991, there were few quantitative restrictions on imports, although licences were required for private sector imports. Botswana's membership of the Southern African Customs Union Agreement (SACUA) also ensured that grain imports were not subject to tariffs (Lado 2001).

Rather than promoting food self-sufficiency through trade controls, the government has instead invested heavily in domestic crop production. The case of Botswana has been quite unusual in the degree to which the government has invested in the agricultural sector. The level of government spending on agricultural support schemes has reached over 40 per cent of agricultural GDP, compared with a more common figure of 4 per cent in other countries (Thirtle et al. 2003). This level of investment has only been possible because of the country's diamond revenues, and represents government attempts to share some of these revenues with the rural sector. In the drive for food self-sufficiency, smallholders were provided with inputs, such as seeds and fertilisers, and with assistance in land preparation and development; considerable public sector resources were devoted to research and extension; and there was large-scale investment in agricultural marketing infrastructure (Lado 2001; Seleka 1999).

Cereal sector policy was implemented by the Botswana Agricultural Marketing Board (BAMB), which was established in 1974 to undertake grain and input marketing activities. BAMB depots were located throughout the country and transport costs were subsidised in an effort to support producer prices and encourage production. Particular emphasis was given to supporting the producer price of sorghum, which – for producers able to deliver to BAMB depots – were twice as high as in neighbouring countries (Lado 2001). Between the late 1980s and 1992, BAMB was given monopoly control over sorghum imports, in a brief departure from the otherwise liberal import regime. The purpose of this, presumably, was to protect the international price differential. However, by this time domestic demand for sorghum was declining in favour of cheaper substitutes, especially imported maize.

The government's focus on cereal production has been criticised for being exceedingly costly in fiscal terms, for its harmful effects on the environment, and for failing to achieve the desired outcome – namely, food self-sufficiency (Lado 2001; Thirtle et al. 2003). Botswana's potential for actually achieving food self-sufficiency appears to be very low because of the country's agro-climatic conditions. Figure 9 shows how, despite large investments in cereal production, cereal imports rose steeply during the 1980s.

Figure 9: Botswana – net imports of cereals

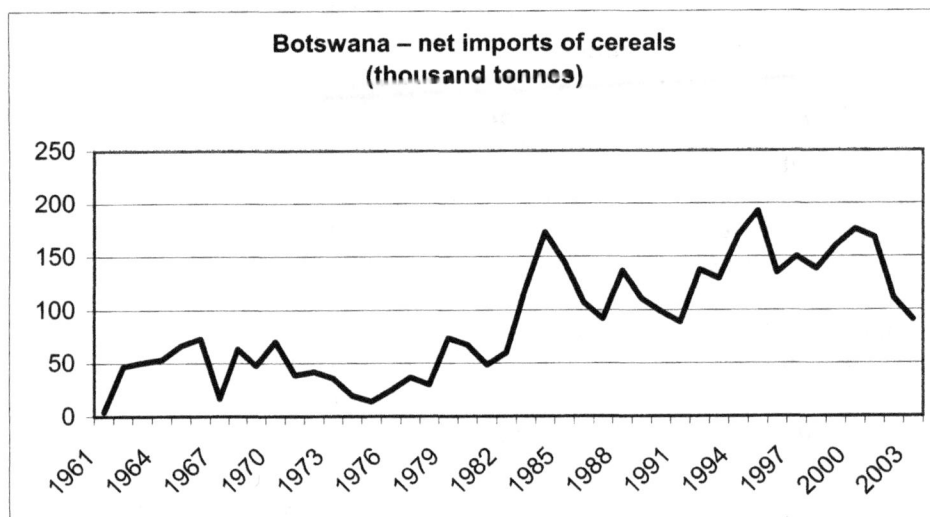

Botswana – net imports of cereals
(thousand tonnes)

Source: FAO 2004

In recognition of the criticisms, the policy of food self-sufficiency was replaced in 1991 with a food security policy. The new policy stressed the need for diversification within the rural sector and shifted the focus of attention from raising cereal production to raising rural incomes. The latter was to be achieved through initiatives aimed at diversifying sources of rural incomes, both within and outside the agricultural sector.

The beef sector

A central feature of policy in the beef sector has been the state's monopoly over exports, which has been implemented by the Botswana Meat Commission (BMC). The role of the BMC in Botswana's beef sector is widely regarded as having been critical to the sector's success in overseas markets, especially in the EU, which is the main importer of Botswana's beef. The BMC, in contrast with many marketing boards in sub-Saharan Africa, appears to be an example of good management and effective state intervention (Stevens and Kennan 2005; Abbott 1987). The strength of the government-controlled, single-channel export marketing system has been its ability to maintain the high quality and health-related standards that are required for imports into the EU. It has been suggested that a competitive export marketing system might be less successful in this regard (Stevens and Kennan 2005).

Policy performance

Despite high levels of investment in arable farming, the crop sector has performed poorly over the past two decades. The output of sorghum grew rapidly in the 1970s because of improvements in both yield and harvested area. However, in the 1980s and 1990s average yields were lower than in the 1960s and 1970s and, although the harvested area continued to grow, total output levelled off at about two-thirds of the 1970s level (see Table 12).

Table 12: Botswana sorghum production

Average annual production indicators	1961–70	1971–80	1981–90	1991–2000
Area (1,000 ha)	85	91	114	119
Output (1,000 mt)	23	40	28	29
Yield (mt/ha)	0.3	0.4	0.2	0.2
% growth in relation to previous decade				
Area		8	24	5
Output		76	-30	5
Yield		63	-44	0

Source: FAO 2004

The area devoted to maize production was very small during the 1960s but grew rapidly in the 1970s, as did output and yields. However, in the following two decades performance fell far below what had been achieved in the 1970s; and in the 1990s yields dropped below their 1960s level (see Table 13).

Table 13: Botswana maize production

Average annual production indicators	1961–70	1971–80	1981–90	1991–2000
Area (1,000 ha)	18	45	25	48
Output (1,000 mt)	6	24	9	10
Yield (mt/ha)	0.3	0.5	0.4	0.2
% growth in relation to previous decade				
Area		158	-44	89
Output		326	-62	7
Yield		65	-32	-44

Source: FAO 2004

The economic return on government investment in the cereal sector has clearly been disappointing. It has been estimated that the total value of output in the sector between 1985 and 1991 was significantly lower than government expenditure over the same period on the Accelerated Rainfed Arable Programme (ARAP) – a programme targeted specifically at boosting national cereal production (Lado 2001). According to a study by Seleka (1999), ARAP did raise yields and output over and above what they would have been without such support, but at a very large fiscal cost.

Despite recent stagnation, the beef sector is generally much stronger than the cereal sector – reflecting the country's comparative advantage in livestock production. Beef production and exports increased rapidly during the 1960s and 1970s, reaching a peak in the mid-1980s. However, the sector did not perform so well in the 1990s, with the average level of production and exports falling back below their 1980s values (see Table 14 and Figure 10.

Table 14: Botswana beef production and trade

Average annual production indicators	1961–70	1971–80	1981–90	1991–2000
Output (1,000 mt)	23	37	42	40
Exports (1,000 mt)	10	30	31	22
Export value (US$m — constant 2000 values)	14	56	73	62
% growth in relation to previous decade				
Output		63	14	-5
Exports		209	2	-28
Export value		306	30	-15

Source: FAO 2004

Figure 10: Value of beef exports

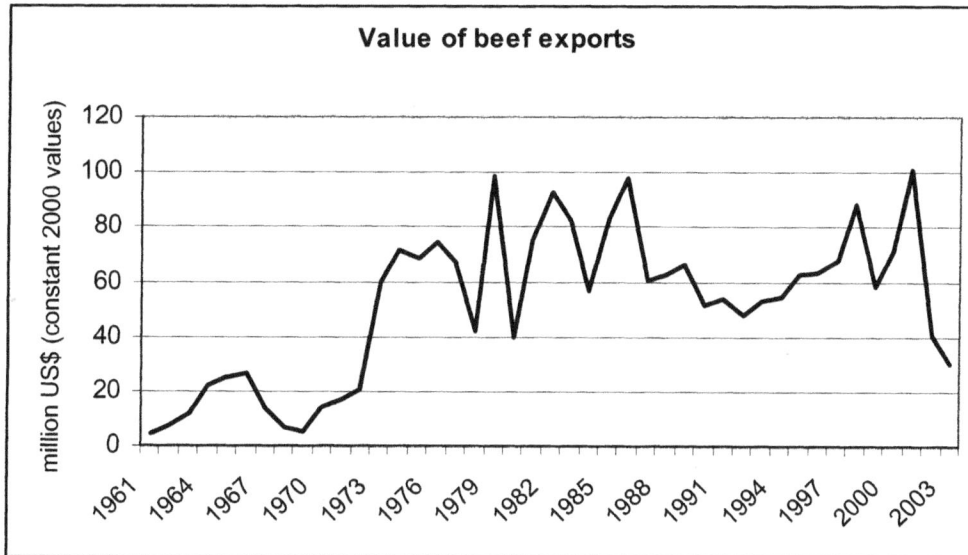

Source: FAO 2004

Poverty

Nationally, the proportion of the population living on less than one dollar a day was 33 per cent in 1985 compared with 31 per cent in 1993, according to the World Bank (2005). By contrast, Whiteside (1997) cites a figure of 47 per cent of the population living in poverty in 1993/94, and states that although the proportion of people living in poverty has fallen sharply, the absolute numbers have remained largely unchanged. Despite the uncertainty surrounding national statistics, it is clear that poverty is concentrated in the rural areas.

However, it is debatable as to what extent the rural poor have benefited from government intervention in the agricultural sector, either before or since 1991. According to Whiteside (1997), 'agriculture has failed to provide a route out of severe poverty'. Only 50 per cent of the rural population own cattle and those who do belong mainly to more affluent rural households (Thirtle et al. 2003). As a consequence, government support for the beef sector has been of little direct benefit to the poor (Lado 2001), although some may have benefited indirectly from the increased demand for rural goods and services that support for the beef sector may have generated. The poor's small share in the benefits of beef production partly explains why considerable public sector resources have been devoted to supporting smallholder production in the crop sector.

However, even these programmes may not have been very effective in reaching the most needy. It has been suggested that price support for cereals was of little benefit to the rural poor, because few of them produce a marketable surplus (Whiteside 1997) and that agricultural support programmes aimed at increasing the productivity – and hence the marketable surplus – of smallholders have failed to reverse the decline in output and yields (Seleka 1999; Moepeng [no date]). According to Lado (2001), large farmers with better access to resources have been the main beneficiaries of government programmes to support arable farming. Despite rapid growth in GDP, achieved largely through the country's successful exploitation of its mineral resources, poverty in the rural areas is a problem that appears stubbornly resistant to change.

Bibliography

Abbott, J. (1987) *Agricultural Marketing Enterprises for the Developing World*, Cambridge University Press.

Adelman, I. and Robinson, S. (1978) *Income Distribution Policy: A computable general equilibrium model of South Korea*, Stanford University Press.

Ahmed, R. and Goletti, F. (1997) 'Food Policy and Market Reform in Viet Nam and Bangladesh', in IFPRI Annual Report 1997, Washington DC: International Food Policy Research Institute.

Arudsothy, P. (1975) 'Malaysia', in Ichimura (1975) (see below).

Benjamin, D. and Brandt, L. (2001) 'Agriculture and Income Distribution in Rural Vietnam under Economic Reforms: A Tale of Two Regions', Toronto: Department of Economics, University of Toronto.

Berdegué, J. (2002) 'Learning to beat Cochrane's treadmill: public policy, markets and social learning in Chile's small-scale agriculture', in C. Leeuwis and R. Pyburn (eds.) *Wheelbarrows Full of Frogs: Social learning in rural resource management*, Assen: Van Gorcum Ltd.

Byun, H.-Y., Chough, S., and Jeong, K.-J. (1975) 'Korea', in Ichimura (1975).

David, C. and Huang, J. (1996) *Political Economy of Rice Price Protection in Asia*, Chicago: University of Chicago.

Dawe, D. (2001) 'How Far Down the Path to Free Trade? The Importance of Rice Price Stabilization in Developing Asia', *Food Policy* 26(2): 163–75.

Dawe, D. (1995) 'The Macroeconomic Benefits of Stabilizing Food Prices', *The Indonesian Food Journal* 5(10): 43–64.

Diao, X., Dyck, J., Skully, D., Somwaru, A., and Lee, C. (2002) 'Structural Change and Agricultural Protection: Costs of Korean Agricultural Policy, 1975 and 1990', Electronic Report no. 809, Economic Research Service, United States Department of Agriculture.

Ellis, F. (1993) 'Indonesian Rice Marketing Study: Aggregate Rice Market and Role of BULOG', *Indonesian Food Journal* 4(7): 23–37.

FAO (2004) FAOSTAT online database, available at http://faostat.fao.org.

Gulati, A. and Narayanan, S. (2002) 'Rice Trade Liberalisation and Poverty', *Economic and Political Weekly*, December 28.

Hachette, D. and Rozas, M. del P. (1993) 'The Liberalization of the Chilean Agriculture: 1974–1990', Working Paper N° 157, Santiago: Department of Economics, Pontificia Catholic University of Chile.

Healy, S., Pearce, R., and Stockbridge, M. (1998) *The Implications of the Uruguay Round Agreement on Agriculture for Developing Countries – a training manual*, Training Materials for Agricultural Planning 41, Rome: Food and Agriculture Organization.

Hope, K. (1998) 'Development Policy and Economic Performance in Botswana: Lessons for the Transition Economies in Sub-Saharan Africa', *Journal of International Development* 10, 539–54.

Ichimura, S. (1975) *The Economic Development of East and Southeast Asia*, Kyoto: The Center for Southeast Asian Studies.

IFPP – Indonesian Food Policy Program (2002) 'Food Security and Rice Price Policy in Indonesia: Reviewing the Debate', Working Paper no. 12, Bappenas/Departemen Pertanian/USAID/DAI Food Policy Advisory Team.

Islam, R. (2003) 'Revisiting the East Asian Model of Economic Growth and Poverty Reduction: A Labour Market Perspective', Conference Paper, Geneva: Recovery and Reconstruction Department, ILO.

Jenkins, G. and Lai, A. (1991) 'Malaysia', in A.e O. Krueger, M. Schiff, and A. Valdes (eds.), *The Political Economy of Agricultural Pricing Policy*, Vol. 2, Baltimore ML: Johns Hopkins University Press.

Lado, C. (2001) 'Environmental and socio-economic factors behind food security policy strategies in Botswana', *Development Southern Africa* 18(2).

Martin, M. and McDonald, J. (1986) *Food Grain Policy in the Republic of Korea: The Economic Costs of Self-Sufficiency*, Chicago: University of Chicago.

Minot, N. and Goletti, F. R. (2000) 'Market Liberalization and Poverty in Viet Nam', Research Report 114, Washington DC: International Food Policy Research Institute.

Moepeng, P. (no date) 'Food Security, Agricultural Policy & Environmental Interface: An African Perspective — The Case of Botswana', Gabarone: Botswana Institute for Development Policy Analysis.

Moon, P.-Y. and Kang, B.-S. (1991) 'The Republic of Korea', in A.O. Krueger, M. Schiff, and A. Valdés (eds.), *The Political Economy of Agricultural Pricing Policy*, Vol. 2, Baltimore ML: Johns Hopkins University Press.

Muchnik, E. and Camhi, R. (2003) 'Impact of Economic and Trade Policy Reforms on Food Security in Chile', Working Paper, Fundación Chile, Agribusiness Department.

Nguyen, H. and Grote, U. (2004) 'Agricultural Policies In Vietnam: Producer Support Estimates, 1986–2002', Center for Development Research (Zef) Discussion Paper No. 93, Washington DC: International Food Policy Research Institute.

OECD/AfDB (2002) 'Botswana', *African Economic Outlook*, 47–58.

OECD (1999) 'National Policies and Agricultural Trade: Review of Agricultural Policies in Korea', Paris: OECD.

Ryan, J. (1999) 'Assessing The Impact of Rice Policy Changes in Viet Nam and the Contribution of Policy Research', Impact Assessment Discussion Paper No. 8., Washington DC: International Food Policy Research Institute.

Seleka, T. B. (1999) 'The performance of Botswana's traditional arable agriculture: growth rates and the impact of the accelerated rainfed arable programme (ARAP)', *Agricultural Economics* 20:121–33.

Siamwalla, A. (2001) 'The Political Economy of Foodgrain and Fertilizer Distribution', in *The Evolving Roles of the State, Private, and Local Actors in Rural Asia*, Study of Rural Asia: Volume 5, Oxford: Oxford University Press.

Stevens, C. and Kennan, J. (2005) 'Botswana Beef Exports and Trade Policy', discussion paper, Brighton: Institute of Development Studies, University of Sussex.

Timmer, C.P. (2000) 'Agriculture and economic development', in B.L. Gardner and G.C Rausser (eds.), *Handbook of Agricultural Economics*, Oxford: Elsevier Science.

Timmer, C. P. (2002a) 'Food Security in an Era of Decentralization: Historical Lessons and Policy Implications for Indonesia', Indonesian Food Policy Program, Working Paper No. 7, Bappenas/USAID/DAI Food Policy Advisory Team.

Timmer, C.P. (2002b) 'Food Security and Rice Price Policy in Indonesia: The Economics and Politics of the Food Price Dilemma', Indonesian Food Policy Program, Working Paper No. 14, Bappenas/ Departemen Pertanian/USAID/DAI Food Policy Advisory Team.

Thirtle, C., Piesse, J., Lusigi, A., and Suhariyanto, K. (2003) 'Multi-factor agricultural productivity, efficiency and convergence in Botswana, 1981–1996', *Journal of Development Economics* 71, 605– 24.

Valdés, A., Hurtado, H., and Muchnik, E. (1991) 'Chile', in A. O. Krueger, M. Schiff, and A. Valdes (eds.), *The Political Economy of Agricultural Pricing Policy*, Vol. 2, Baltimore ML: Johns Hopkins University Press.

Vietnam Development Report (2004) 'Poverty', Vietnam Development Report 2004, Hanoi: Vietnam Development Information Center.

Wawn, B. (1982) *The Economies of the ASEAN Countries*, Oxford: Macmillan.

Whiteside, M. (1997) 'Encouraging Sustainable Family Sector Agriculture In Botswana', Agricultural Services Reform In Southern Africa (R6452ca), Stroud: Environment and Development Consultancy Ltd and Gabarone: Co-operation for Research, Development & Education (CORDE).

World Bank (2005) 'World Bank Development Indicators', available at https://publications.worldbank.org/WDI/.

World Bank (1993) *The East Asian Miracle: Economic Growth and Public Policy*, Oxford: Oxford University Press

WTO (2004) 'WTO Agriculture Negotiations: the issues and where we are now', www.wto.org.